Recreating Historic Dress

Recreating Historic Dress: Clothing Gems from the Hereford Museum Clothing Collection, with Patterns compiles patterns and information for 25 never-before-published garments from the historic clothing collection at the Hereford Museum and Art Gallery Resource Centre, Hereford, UK.

An accurate study of dress is dependent on the very close and careful examination of existing garments. Nancy Hills has conducted a detailed analysis of a range of garments, spanning the years 1755 through to 1954, carefully exploring what they can tell us and translating them into paper patterns. Each featured garment contains a detailed description, the pattern, historical context, and images of the full article of clothing and construction details from inside the garment. This book features an eclectic selection of clothing, including a comfortable 18th-century cotton caraco often worn for work, leisure, travel, or pregnancy, a simple cotton print dress worn in 1834 as a wedding dress, and two dresses, one from 1936 and one from 1954, that show a more elite pedigree, with their labels of popular London designers.

This book will be of interest to experienced costume designers and technicians, cutters and drapers, intermediate students of theatrical costume design, and historical reenactors.

Nancy E. Hills is a Full Professor at Utah State University, where she is head of the Theatre Costume Design program. Shows featuring her period piece designs include *Les Liaisons Dangereuses, Pride and Prejudice, To Kill a Mockingbird, The Miser, Enchanted April, Our Country's Good, Emma, Much Ado About Nothing, Anna Karenina, A Christmas Carol, The Moors, Pericles,* and *Misalliance*. In 2013, Nancy gave a TEDxTalk on the impact of WWII on clothing called *Make Do and Mend* and was the recipient of the Janet Arnold Award from the Society of Antiquaries in London.

Scott Nicklas is a graphic designer at Sports Training Systems in Portland, Oregon, where he specializes in developing educational materials for international gymnastics judges around the world. An Oregon State University graduate with a BFA in Graphic Design, in 2014 Scott designed graphic displays for Nancy's exhibits at the Society of Antiquaries, including *Symphony in White*, *Shades of White*, and *More Shades of White*.

Recreating Historic Dress

Clothing Gems from the Hereford Museum Clothing Collection, with Patterns

Nancy E. Hills

Routledge
Taylor & Francis Group
NEW YORK AND LONDON

Designed cover image: Photo by Nancy E. Hills. Cover design by Scott Nicklas.

First published 2025
by Routledge
605 Third Avenue, New York, NY 10158

and by Routledge
4 Park Square, Milton Park, Abingdon, Oxon, OX14 4RN

Routledge is an imprint of the Taylor & Francis Group, an informa business

ISBN: 978-1-032-62461-7 (hbk)
ISBN: 978-1-032-62458-7 (pbk)
ISBN: 978-1-032-62463-1 (ebk)

DOI: 10.4324/9781032624631

Typeset in Garamond Premier Pro, Minion Pro, and Myriad Pro
by Scott Nicklas

Publisher's Note
This book has been prepared from camera-ready copy provided by the author.

Contents

Introduction

Illustrations, paintings, and statues are a great source of information about the history of clothing. 19th-century daguerreotypes provide sharp, individual images of period dress. Actual surviving garments reveal even more. Clothing design is an art that relates closely to the personal narratives of our lives. It is an individual expression of style. It is intensely personal and at the same time a reflection of the state of society. Molded by the body that wore it, wrinkled by years of use, carefully hand-stitched, and stained from 200-year-old perspiration, clothing is the most intimately human of the surviving decorative arts. A garment is a visual and tactile biography of its wearer. The artist, William Hogarth, believed it was possible to "know the very minds of the people by their dress."

My name is Nancy E. Hills and I am the head of the Theatre Costume Design program at the Caine College of the Arts at Utah State University (USU). Among my teaching responsibilities is the study of historic dress.

In 2013, I was honored to receive the Janet Arnold Award from the Society of Antiquaries in London. Janet Arnold was an artist, teacher, costume designer, and conservator. The Society funded the Janet Arnold Award to further in-depth study of Western dress. Her skills and her focus on period accuracy turned the study of historic clothing into a serious discipline.

When I was a university student, I was introduced to Janet Arnold's *Patterns of Fashion*. They became the foundation of my knowledge of historic patterns. During graduate school studying theatre costume design, the very top of my Christmas wish list was Arnold's *Queen Elizabeth's Wardrobe Unlock'd*. My mother got me that book. It has been an important part of my personal library ever since. Every costume shop I have worked in has a set of Arnold's *Patterns of Fashion*. I can look through my costume stock at the Utah State Theatre and identify which garments were influenced by the patterns from all those books. There are many.

As part of the grant from the Society of Antiquaries, I developed patterns from existing garments from two clothing collections in the United Kingdom. One is the Snowshill Collection (well represented in Arnold's books) and housed at Berrington Hall near Leominster in Herefordshire. This collection was developed by the English architect, artist, craftsman, and poet, Charles Paget Wade, whose other collections are housed at Snowshill Manor in Gloucestershire.

The other collection is in the Hereford Museum and Art Gallery housed in the Hereford Museum Resource Centre. At that time, textile historian, Althea Mackenzie, was the curator of both of these collections. Her historic expertise was another extraordinary resource for me.

I first met Althea Mackenzie in Herefordshire, when Utah State University Faculty member, Darrin Brookes and I were doing research for our presentation on 18th century interiors and clothing titled *Big Hair, Big Chair.*

An accurate study of dress is dependent on a very close examination of existing garments. I have now done a detailed analysis of over 50 garments, carefully exploring what they can tell us and translating them into paper patterns. I originally chose 11 garments and recreated them in monochromatic white mockups. Those garments were modeled by USU students at a talk I gave at the Society of Antiquaries in London. They were later placed on exhibit at Berrington Hall in Herefordshire as *Symphony in White.* That original group has grown to 40 garments and shown in public displays in Hereford, at the United States Institute for Theatre (USITT), The Society of Antiquaries, and at USU including, *Shades of White, Histories Mysteries, Unearthing the Past,* and *More Shades of White.* Every piece has provided me with interesting insights and posed challenging questions.

This book includes details of 25 of these garments, all from the Hereford Museum and Art Gallery Resource Centre Collection. I have included a description of the garment, the pattern I created, a historical context for each, and images of the original pieces. I hope you enjoy exploring these garments and their construction and history, as much as I have.

Most of the garments are stored in drawers wrapped in acid free paper or in acid free boxes with acid-free paper. The drawers and shelves are in moving wall storage units. These garments have been collected for more than a century. Some of them have a notation with information about the donor.

When available I have included that information in the descriptions.

I have been collecting patterns for about a decade. I originally chose garments that I personally liked and eventually I chose ones that filled in the gaps with the approximately 200-year span.

I have extracted over 60+ patterns. In the 18th century, cutting into fabric was only done if necessary. Most skirts in the 18th and first half of the 19th centuries were made with the full width of the fabric sewed selvage to selvage. The skirts are usually pleated and sewed onto the bodice. Fuller skirts are knife-pleated or cartridge-pleated. If you could achieve a style line from folding the fabric into a deep seam, this was often done. It seems there was a reluctance to cut into fabric. It would certainly make it easier to repurpose a garment when this load of uncut fabric was available.

After I study a garment, I draw each pattern piece in a small-scale format trying to determine the scale of each piece in relation to the other pieces. I then take careful measurements with the garment placed on a dress form. Please note, since seam allowance varies depending on personal practice and a need to not cut into fabric. I don't include seam allowance in any of my patterns.

With the garment placed on a dress form, I redraw the pattern pieces in full scale, taking all measurements from the actual garment using my small pattern drawing as a checkoff list.

Most of these garments are small in size and short in height compared to today's average size. They are generally 5'3" in height.

I spend hours on each pattern piece, measuring, redrawing the pattern piece, finding the placement of the style lines, determining the grain line, finding the selvage edges, etc. When I find the selvage edges, I can determine the width of the original yardage.

Selvage measurements became complicated with the intricacies of style during the post-crinoline periods and returned again with the simplicities of cut during the First World War. The only creative liberties I take are where I cannot see the exact shape of a difficult seamed area. I use my best judgement under these circumstances. I also true up the patterns so they can fit together like a puzzle rather than a garment that has been stretched from years of use.

I find the most interesting garments are the ones that you can see the alterations and adjustments for updating an out of fashion garment. I first noticed this in the 1750 pink wool riding habit. There is a discussion of the contemporary alterations done on that garment.

When I make one of these patterns into a garment and put it in my white dresses collection, I start with the original pattern and adjust them to the size I need them to be. In the case of the white dresses, most of the dress forms I have are an American size 6, so I make the white dresses size 6. When I use them for a play I am designing, I adjust the sizes accordingly. All of these patterns are the actual size of the garment in the Hereford Museum.

When using these patterns, each square represents one square inch regardless of its physical size.

Professor Nancy E. Hills
Costume Designer
Theatre Arts Department
Caine College of the Arts
Utah State University, Logan, Utah

The Collection

The Hereford Museum and Art Gallery Costume Collection housed in the Museum Resource Centre in Hereford, UK, is at the heart of this volume.

The costume collection is of local, regional, and national significance. Most of the collection has been locally donated. There have been significant donations by The Friends of Hereford Museum and Art Galleries. Among other significant donations are several items from C. W. Cunnington, who extensively studied the collection for his publications on the history of costume.

"The costume collection consists of women's, men's and children's costume and accessories, civil and military uniforms, textiles, and a small amount of foreign costume. Women's costume includes - a large collection of dresses dating from the first half of the 18th century to present day. The 18th and early 19th century is very well represented in terms of dresses and accessories. These include:-aprons, blouses, bodices, bonnets (soft) and hats (one rare fine split straw hat reputedly belonging to Queen Anne), boots and bottines, bustles, capes, cape shawls, shawl pelerines, cloaks and mantles, coats, collars and cuffs, corsetry, drawers, combinations, crinolines, dressing gowns and jackets, fichus, fronts and shirts, gloves, mittens and muffs, housecaps, jackets and boleros, nightwear, pattens, pellises, petticoats, riding habits, shawls, shoes, skirts, sleeves, slippers, stockings, underbodices and chemises, veils and hats, dress patterns, belts, bracelets, brooches, buckles, buttons, card cases, chatelaines, combs, dress holders, ear ornaments, fans, head ornaments, fobs, garters, handbags, handkerchiefs, hat-pins, links and studs, lockets and pendants, materials and trimmings, muffs, necklaces, parasols, pockets, purses, rings, scarves, scent bottles, seals, spectacles, sticks, umbrellas, wig curlers and wig stands, glove stretchers, hair curlers, snuff boxes and shawl fasteners."

— Althea Mackenzie

Retired Curator
Historic Clothing Collection
Hereford Museum and Art Gallery

1750

Wool Riding Habit

In the 18th century, country life revolved around the seasons. From planting to harvest, estate owners, both aristocracy and landed gentry, remained in the country and tended their land. Social activities began after the needs of the land were met. The social season revolved around urban social agendas and the political business of Parliament.

In 1750, any well-appointed lady would have a riding habit. In addition to equestrian pursuits, riding habits were increasingly worn for travel and informal outdoor leisure wear. Constructed by tailors, they were expensive to make and trim. They consisted of a man's style tailored coat, often with two skirts; one ankle length for walking and one longer for riding side saddle. This garment shows the shorter walking length skirt. This riding habit was likely worn with a lightweight foundation garment, less boned than stays. That garment may have been riding stays (lightly boned) or a jump (cord quilted). Both of these garments would have been worn over a linen shift.

Active country living is well represented by this riding habit. The striking pink jacket and skirt have style lines and decoration that echo men's wear. The collar, lapels, and pocket flaps have the same types of decoration as a man's coat of the period. Made of pink calamanco wool, it has metallic silver buttons and braid inspired from the military. A three-cornered tricorn hat was likely worn with this ensemble.

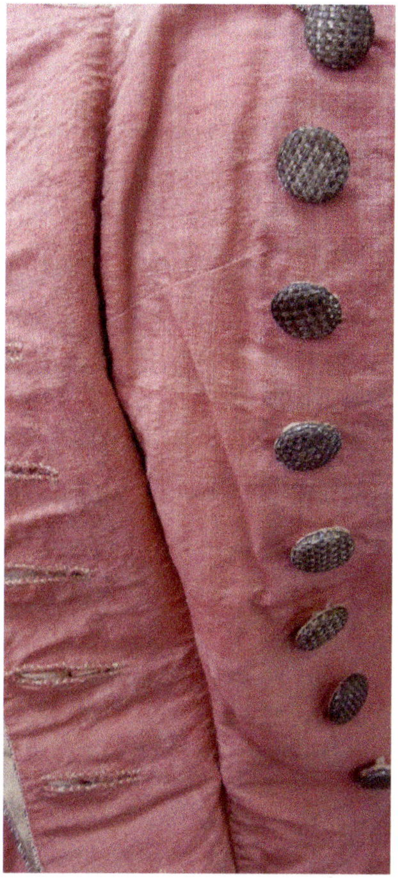

Revers unbuttoned

This garment shows signs of modification and modernizing. Many of the dresses in the Hereford collection have alterations in style or size. A well-trained lady's maid or a practical housewife would often make or remake clothes. Making over and renovating garments was commonplace, whatever the income or social level. When cost was not a concern, the accessibility of materials may have been. When an 18th century person looked at an out-of-style garment they did not think of it as too old-fashioned but rather how they could harvest the fabric and make something new.

Flare taken out of cuff

The jacket has matching revers and is piped with burnished silver cord. The revers have horizontal burnished silver buttonholes and covered buttons. There is a horizontal dart a third down the center front of the jacket that gives a curve to the front closure to fit over an 18th century set of stays. The skirt of the jacket is made of four gored pieces, separately bag lined. The center back jacket skirt pieces overlap and are decorated with three loops of silver piping. This loop arrangement creates a design at the top of the overlap. The skirt side seams also overlap and are held in place with decorative buttonholes and buttons. The side seams overlap at the waist and it also has the looped silver cord (see Skirt Back on pattern page). Both loops of cord nest a silver button. The center back waist overlap may have once had a similar decorative button.

The skirt consists of six waist-to-floor, 15-inch-wide panels. The four panels in the back are knife pleated toward the center, which finishes in a box pleat in the center back. The front consists of two panels. One of these appears to have been reduced in width 4½ inches. The skirt is tied at the side waist with twill tape drawstrings.

The curved two-piece sleeves are finished with narrow cuffs. These cuffs appear to have been updated from an earlier style. Other cuffs from jackets of this kind are usually wider and have some flair. The wider flared cuffs would have fitted in with the older style of the rest of the jacket. The cuffs are 4½ inches wide and sit close to the bottom of the sleeve. I believe the cuffs were made from part of the 4½-inch strip removed from the front skirt panel.

The outside edges of the revers, the two rows on the collar, the edges of the pocket flaps, the center front, the center back, and the cuffs are all piped with silver cord. The jacket collar and skirt are bag lined with cream linen.

The Hereford Collection dates the garment from 1775 but the main part of the riding habit conforms to earlier styles. The 1750 date in the title is an approximation.

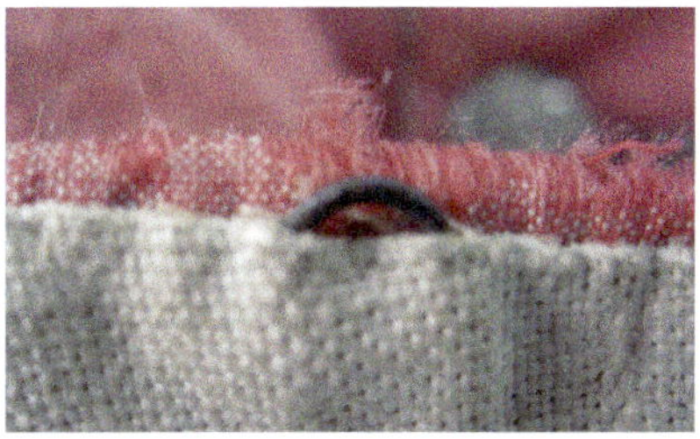

Close-up of eye

Skirt back

Pocket flap

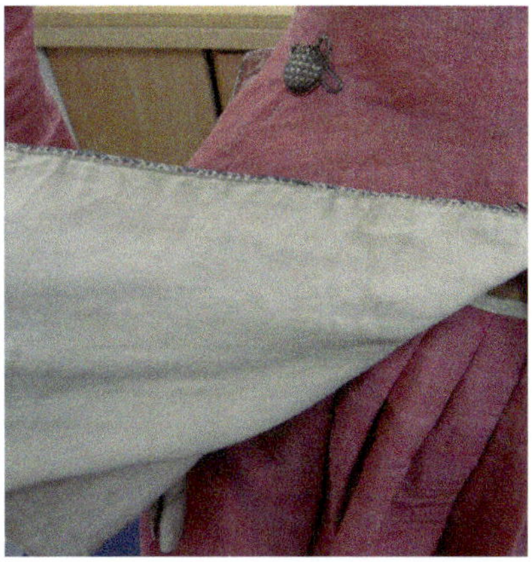

Skirt back detail

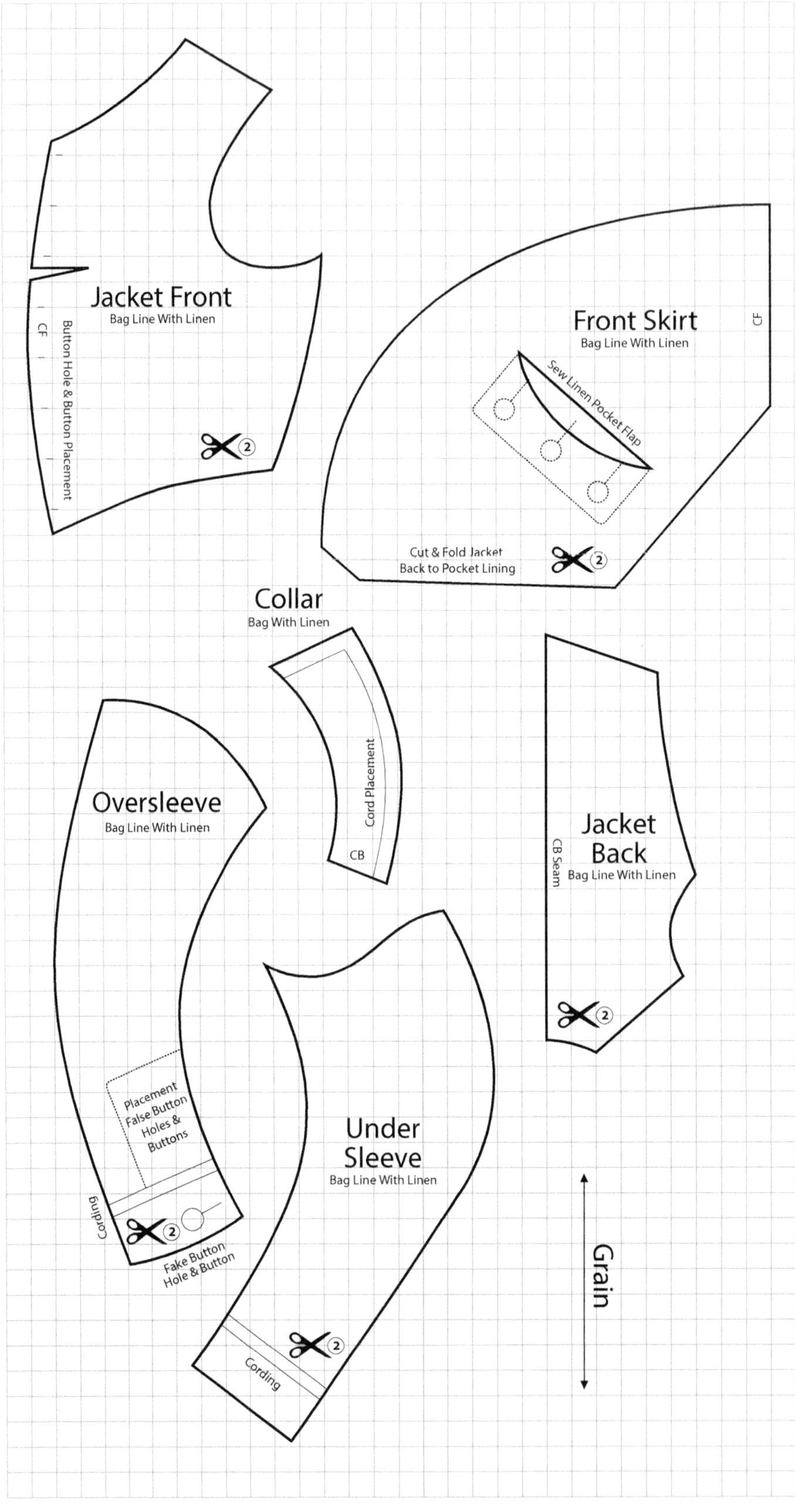
Jacket Front
Bag Line With Linen
CF
Button Hole & Button Placement
2
Front Skirt
Bag Line With Linen
CF
Sew Linen Pocket Flap
Cut & Fold Jacket
Back to Pocket Lining
2
Collar
Bag With Linen
Cord Placement
CB
Jacket
Back
Bag Line With Linen
CB Seam
2
Oversleeve
Bag Line With Linen
Placement
False Button
Holes &
Buttons
Cording
2
Fake Button
Hole & Button
Under
Sleeve
Bag Line With Linen
2
Cording
Grain

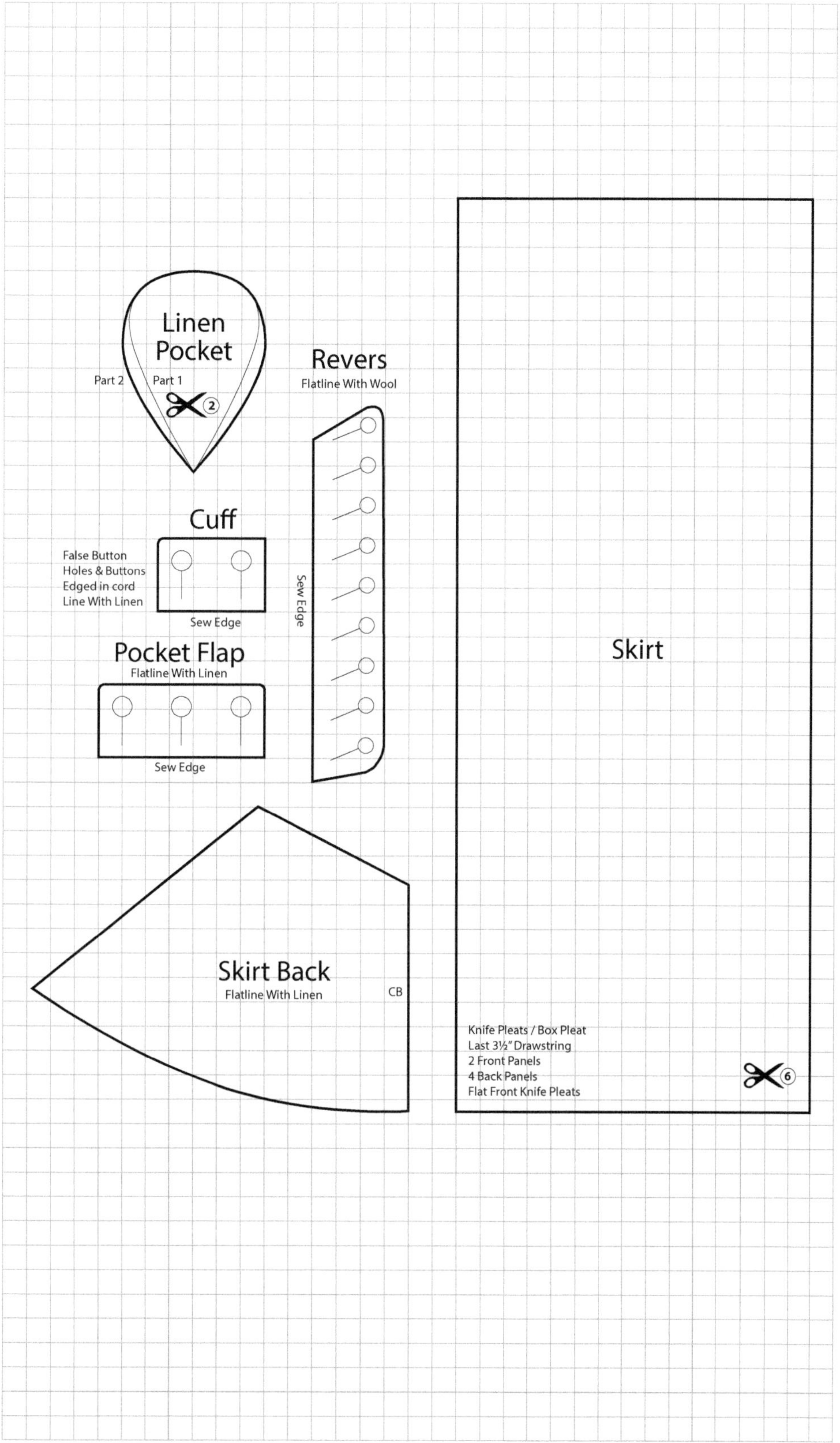
Linen Pocket
Part 2
Part 1
2
Revers
Flatline With Wool
Cuff
False Button
Holes & Buttons
Edged in cord
Line With Linen
Sew Edge
Sew Edge
Pocket Flap
Flatline With Linen
Sew Edge
Skirt
Skirt Back
Flatline With Linen
CB
Knife Pleats / Box Pleat
Last 3½" Drawstring
2 Front Panels
4 Back Panels
Flat Front Knife Pleats
6

1760

Silk Brocade Sack-Back

The sack-back gown was developed from the late 17th-century mantua. Whale-bone or wicker conical hoops were reintroduced to women's skirt shapes in the 1710s. By the 1720s a mantua was worn over a bell-shaped hoop, not unlike the shape of St. Paul's cathedral. The mantua dress was originally fit across the back with several tightly-formed pleats. Innovative change in the sack-backs were the pleats that were unstitched and became a series of shoulder-to-floor box pleats. The effect was that of a matching cape.

This grey-green gown has petite side fullness. In addition to the sack-back, the side of this gown may have been held out with modestly sized side hoops or hip pads. The woman who wore this garment would have worn a set of stays which slimmed the torso. This graceful pyramid would have been majestic, powerful, and conservative; tasteful rather than elaborate.

This gown is constructed with two different weaves of embroidered silks of similar color. Rococo fashion influenced these silks, with heavy swirling brocade and simple flower motifs. The bodice and sleeves are constructed from one of these. The bodice and sleeve fabric has a pattern of large squares, flanked by simple flowers

Back neck

Skirt knife pleats

Side

with more elaborate flowers in the center of each square. The sack-back, skirt, and sleeve flounces are the swirling brocade. It is the same grey-green, but with a large pattern, organic floral.

The bodice includes an attached matching stomacher that closes at the center front with hooks and loop eyes. The stomacher is decorated with two serpentine pieces of ruching sewn to the stomacher from neck to waist. The bodice is finished with robings center front and ending at the shoulder. Another single piece of bodice fabric is attached, laying across the back of the neck. The sleeves are cut cross the grain with the pattern of large squares. The selvage with a yellow line along its length can be seen at the edge of the elbow of the ¾-length sleeve. A scalloped single sleeve flounce is constructed from the large organic floral

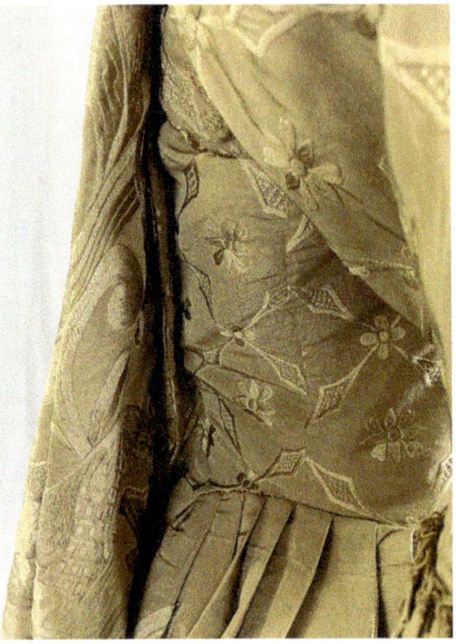

Sack-back

Stomacher gathered ruching

fabric. The flounce is gathered to fit the bottom of the sleeve. There is matching gimp trim along the top of the sleeve flounce and along the bottom edge of the flounce ruffle.

The sack-back pleat is constructed from the second fabric. The pleat is a double inverted box pleat flaring from shoulder to hem. The remainder of the skirt is knife-pleated and attached facing the back of the gown, with a concentration of the knife pleats at the sides. The 10-inch pocket slits are between the front and front side skirt seams.

The bodice is kept snug to the back of the wearer with three rudimentary strips of stabilizing linen. They are attached to the inside and sit across the back of the wearer under the sack pleat.

Back

Pleat stabilizers

Cuff

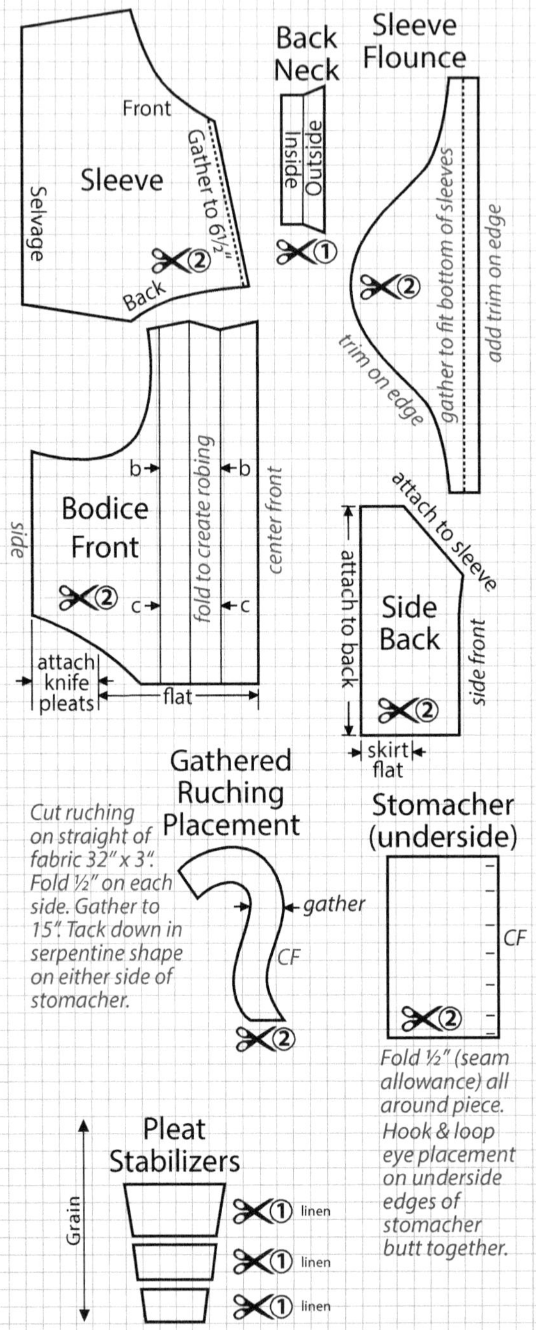
Sleeve
Front
Gather to 6½"
Selvage
Back
Back Neck
Inside
Outside
Sleeve Flounce
gather to fit bottom of sleeves
add trim on edge
trim on edge
Bodice Front
side
fold to create robing
center front
b
c
attach knife pleats
flat
attach to sleeve
attach to back
Side Back
side front
skirt flat
Gathered Ruching Placement
Cut ruching on straight of fabric 32" x 3". Fold ½" on each side. Gather to 15". Tack down in serpentine shape on either side of stomacher.
gather
CF
Stomacher (underside)
CF
Fold ½" (seam allowance) all around piece. Hook & loop eye placement on underside edges of stomacher butt together.
Pleat Stabilizers
Grain
linen
linen
linen

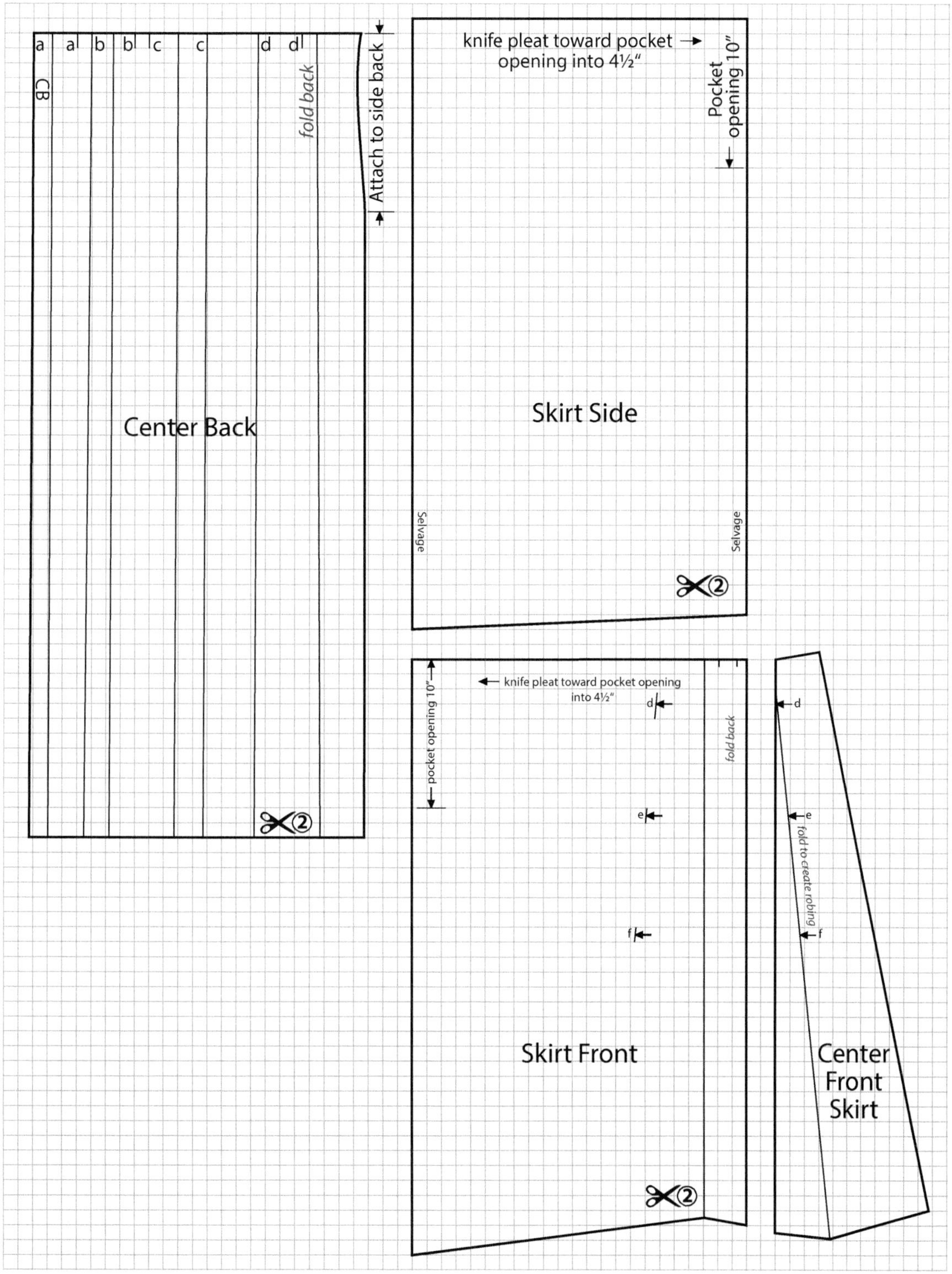

a a b b c c d d
CB
fold back
Attach to side back
Center Back
2
knife pleat toward pocket opening into 4½"
Pocket opening 10"
Skirt Side
Selvage
Selvage
2
pocket opening 10"
knife pleat toward pocket opening into 4½"
d
e
f
fold back
Skirt Front
2
d
e
f
fold to create robing
Center Front Skirt

1775

Cotton Caraco

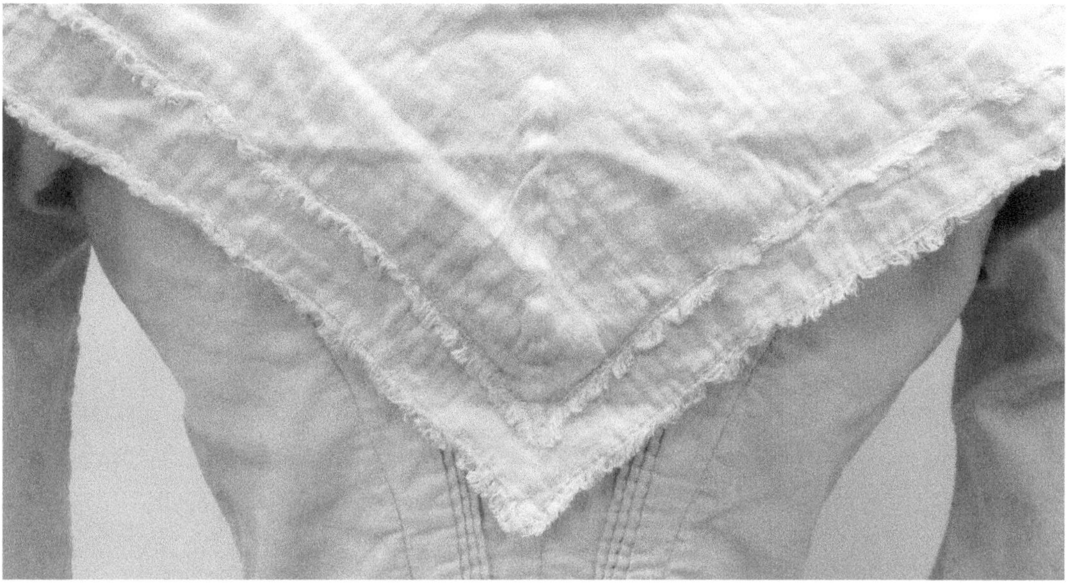

Center back collar

Discoveries made at Pompeii and Herculaneum in the first half of the 18th century fueled a neoclassical revival. This included the decorative and visual arts. It drew inspiration from the art and culture of ancient Greece and Rome. Neoclassicism had its origins in mid-18th-century Rome, but grew in popularity all over Europe and the Americas. At this time, generations of young Europeans took their "Grand Tours" and returned home with Greek and Roman artifacts and ideals.

The artifacts included white marble statuary that inspired many 18th-century artists to create similar work. The popularity of these items influenced a greater use of white in women's clothing. White and cream were also natural standard colors of cotton fabric. Indian calico and muslin began to be copied in England.

Base of back waist

In 1783, in the grounds of Versailles, Marie Antoinette created her Little Hamlet. This was a mock farm complete with farmhouse, dairy, and poultry yard— all for activities traditionally associated with women. When visiting her farm, the Queen and her attendants would dress as shepherdesses and play at being milkmaids. This mania for rural country life coincided with the English affinity for country living.

Cuff with Dorset wheel button

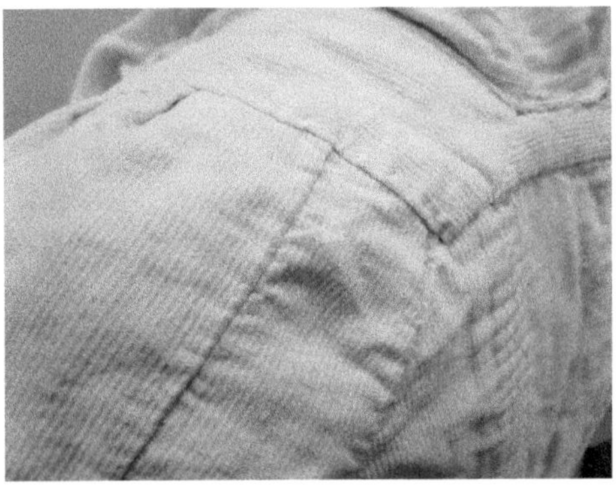

Shoulder panel

By 1770, working-class clothing was worn by women, made with convenience in mind. Women wore a petticoat and a hip-length garment called a short gown, much like a jacket or over-blouse. This cream-colored, cotton caraco evolved from both a working-class and rural short gown that opened in the front. The neck to waist tucks sewed down in the back are a vestige of the sack-back gown from earlier in the century. The gathered drawstrings are adjustable at the center front bust and at the waist. This flexibility made it practical for travel, work, or to accommodate a growing pregnancy.

A lovely detail on this garment is the single Dorset wheel-style button that holds each sleeve cuff closed. Early Dorset wheel buttons were made on a disc cut from the horn of a Dorset sheep. The circle of horn was covered with thread to create the spokes of the wheel. Button makers could later buy metal rings to use as the foundation for these buttons.

This caraco was worn as an informal at-home garment. It was constructed from 32-inch-wide cotton. The front bodice is gathered across the torso with three sets of ties. The center front tie gathers and ties closed at the collar and bodice neck. The second one gathers and ties closed just below the bust. A third tie gathers and closes at the waist. A 3½-inch 3-to-1 ruffle flanks the center front closures and continues around the edge of the skirt hem. The bodice is carefully pleated in the back from neck to waist. The neck is finished with a large collar that is pointed in the back and tucked into the front similar to a fishu.

The sleeves are slightly curved and end just above the wrist. They are finished in a cuff made of a single layer of fabric. The cuff is trimmed with two rows of narrow fringe and closed with one Dorset button.

The caraco skirt is pleated and gathered all around the waist. This gives the skirt nearly a full circle of fullness. This garment would have undoubtedly been worn over a simple petticoat.

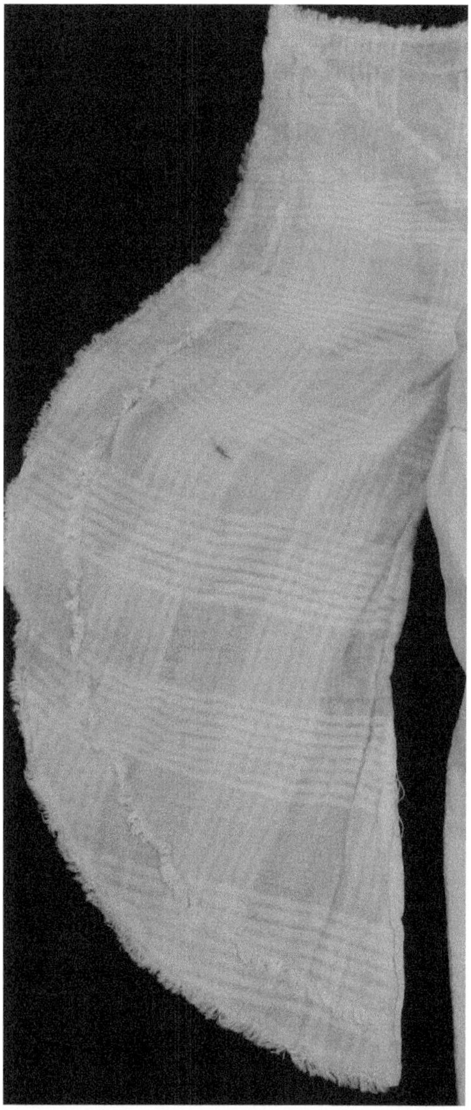

Collar

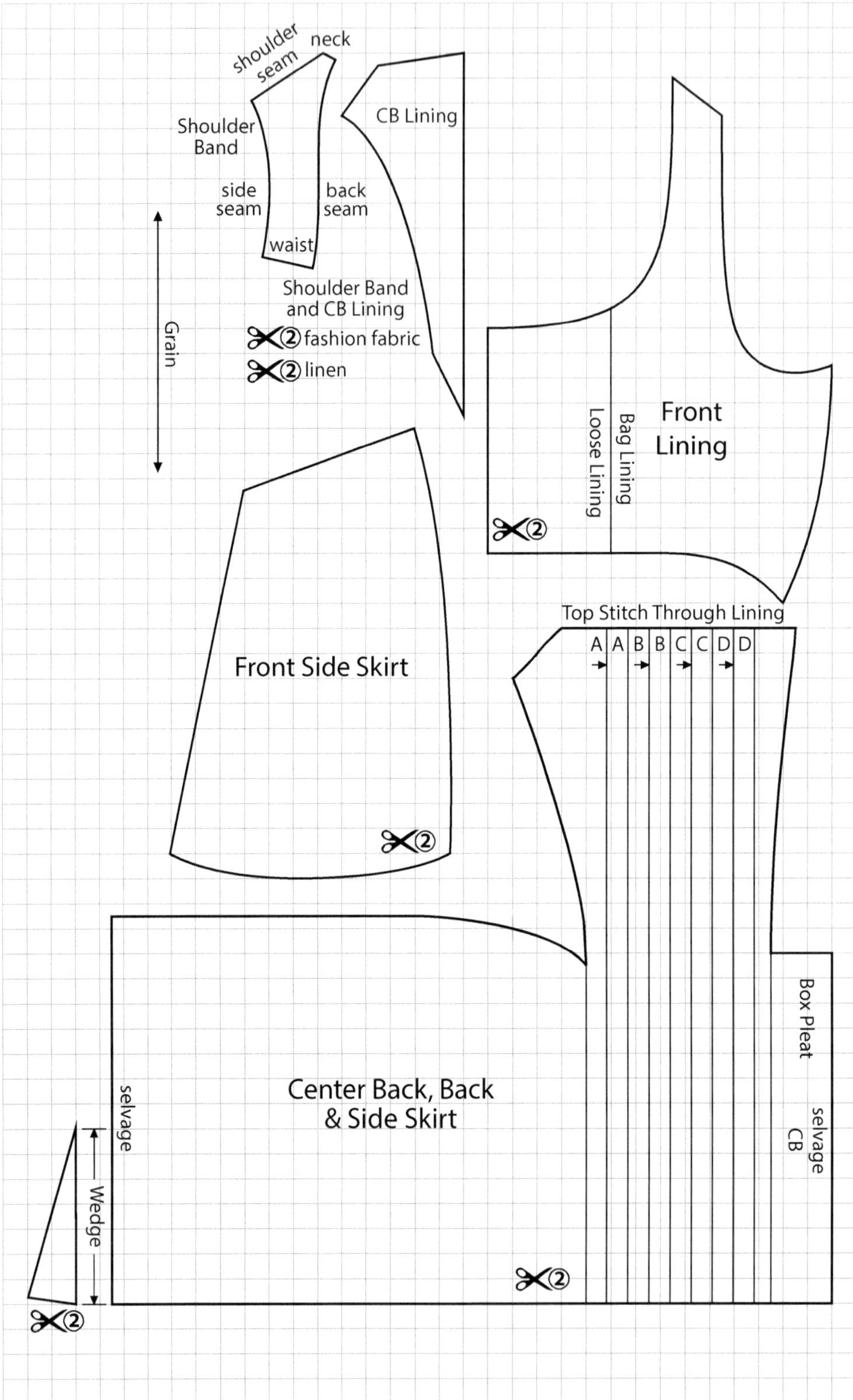
shoulder seam
neck
Shoulder Band
side seam
back seam
waist
CB Lining
Shoulder Band and CB Lining
②fashion fabric
②linen
Grain
Front Lining
Bag Lining
Loose Lining
②
Front Side Skirt
②
Top Stitch Through Lining
A A B B C C D D
Center Back, Back & Side Skirt
selvage
Box Pleat
selvage CB
Wedge
②
②

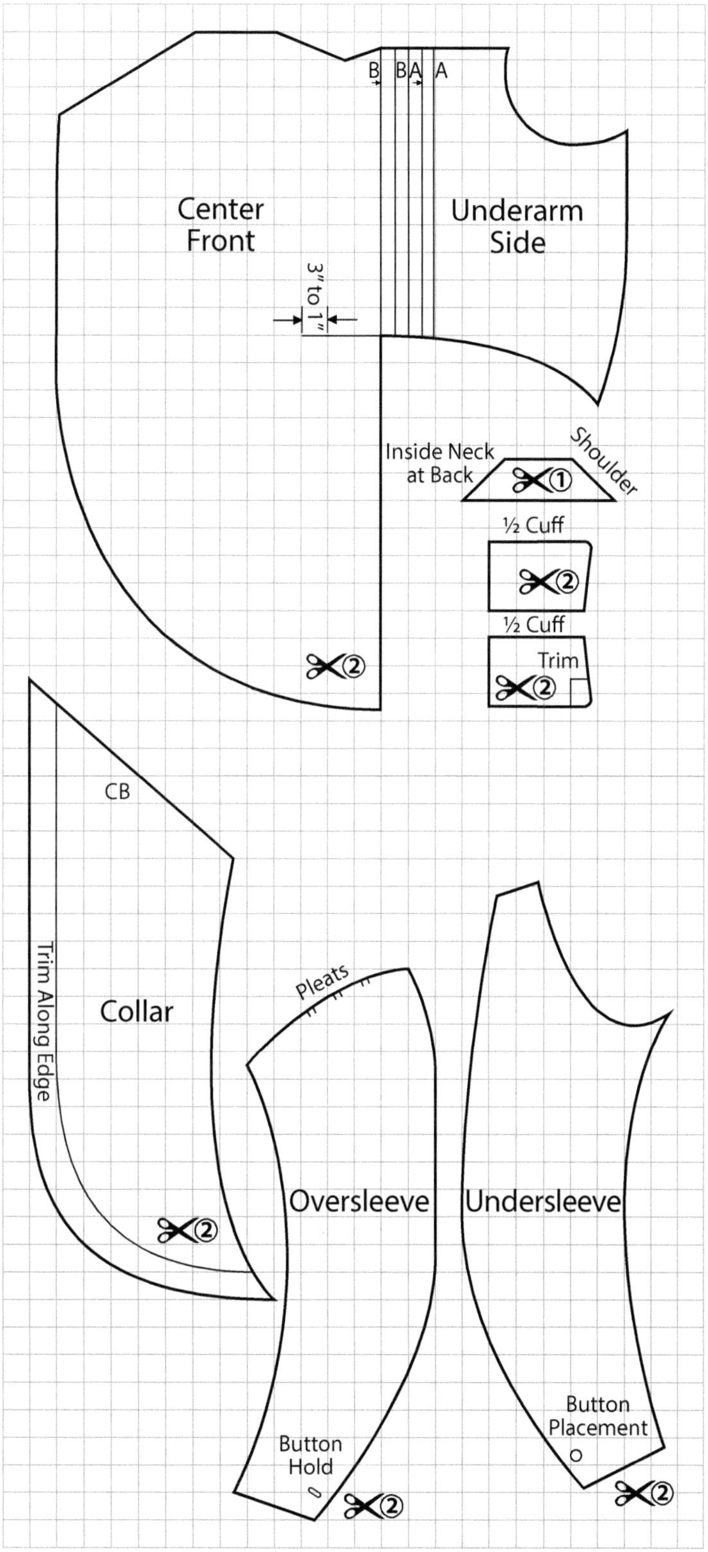

B
B
A
A
Center Front
Underarm Side
3" to 1"
✂②
Inside Neck at Back
Shoulder
✂①
½ Cuff
✂②
½ Cuff
Trim
✂②
CB
Trim Along Edge
Collar
✂②
Pleats
Oversleeve
Undersleeve
Button Hold
✂②
Button Placement
✂②

1780

Grosgrain Polonaise

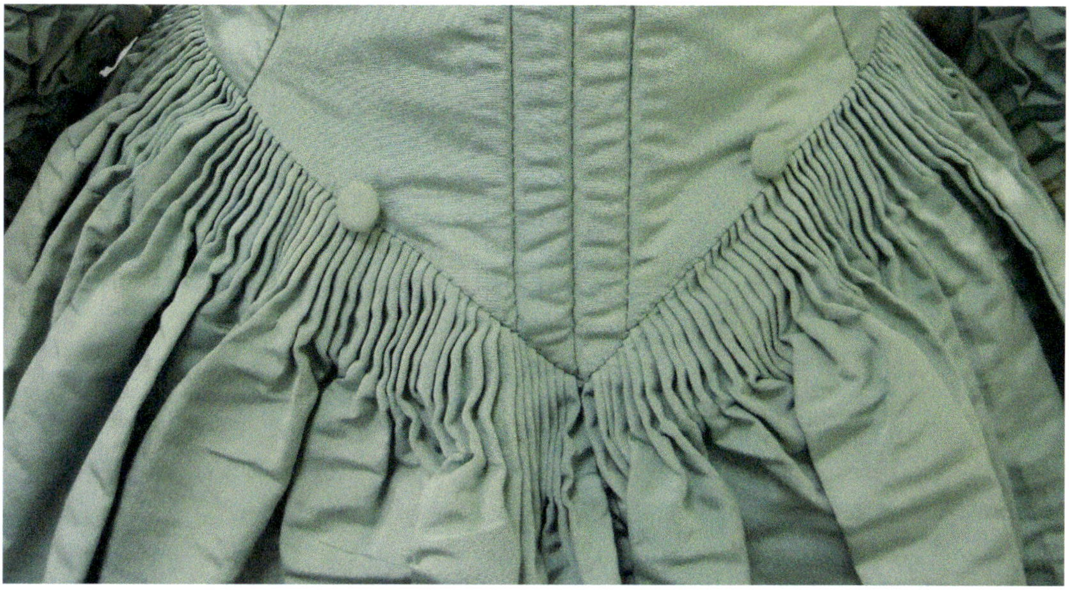

Skirt knife pleats face center back, polonaise buttons

Skirt swaged into polonaise

England prospered during the 18th century, as the businesses expanded all over the world. Imports and exports doubled between the beginning of the century and the 1770s. By the end of the 18th century, the small privileged class of noble families began to allow commoners into their ranks. This wealth-based transformation included many who had gained their money through commerce and banking. This slight democratization of society along with the clean lines of the neoclassical look caused a simplification in clothing style. An Anglomania for country living influenced adaptations in both men's and women's clothing.

Skirt swaged into polonaise, detail

Skirt panel folded hem

By 1780, the new polonaise style was a fashionable variation of that time. Lower- and middle-class women usually wore garments that could be shortened for physical tasks. They used various ways of hiking their overskirts up and out of the muck of the barns, fields, and streets for this work. The skirt was divided into three distinct draped sections called the robe à la Polonaise or Polish style. The Polish reference was to commemorate the 1772 partition of Poland into three territories. One portion went to Prussia, one to Austria, and the third to Russia.

Some skirts were pulled up with two loops under the skirt. Others were pulled up with a long string loop that was sewed into the waist under the skirt and hooked to a button on the outside of the skirt at the back. This very practical draping created a beautiful swaged silhouette.

The Polonaise style of this 1780s eggshell blue silk grosgrain gown is created by the draped overskirt, with the two long drawstrings attached to covered back buttons forming the puffed swags of the stiff silk.

The skirt is knife-pleated into the waist and the combination of the pleats and the triple drape creates a beautiful overskirt. The width of the fabric is 19 inches. There are two red lines woven along the edge of the selvage. Small strips of ruched cream silk ribbon flank the center of the skirt and the neckline. The center front bodice is closed with hooks and eyes and remains unadorned.

The sleeves are simple three-quarter length. Mirroring the swags of the blue grosgrain skirt are the smocked cuffs at the elbow bend of the sleeves. This repeats the simple beauty of manipulating the rich fabric as decoration.

Free-form smocking

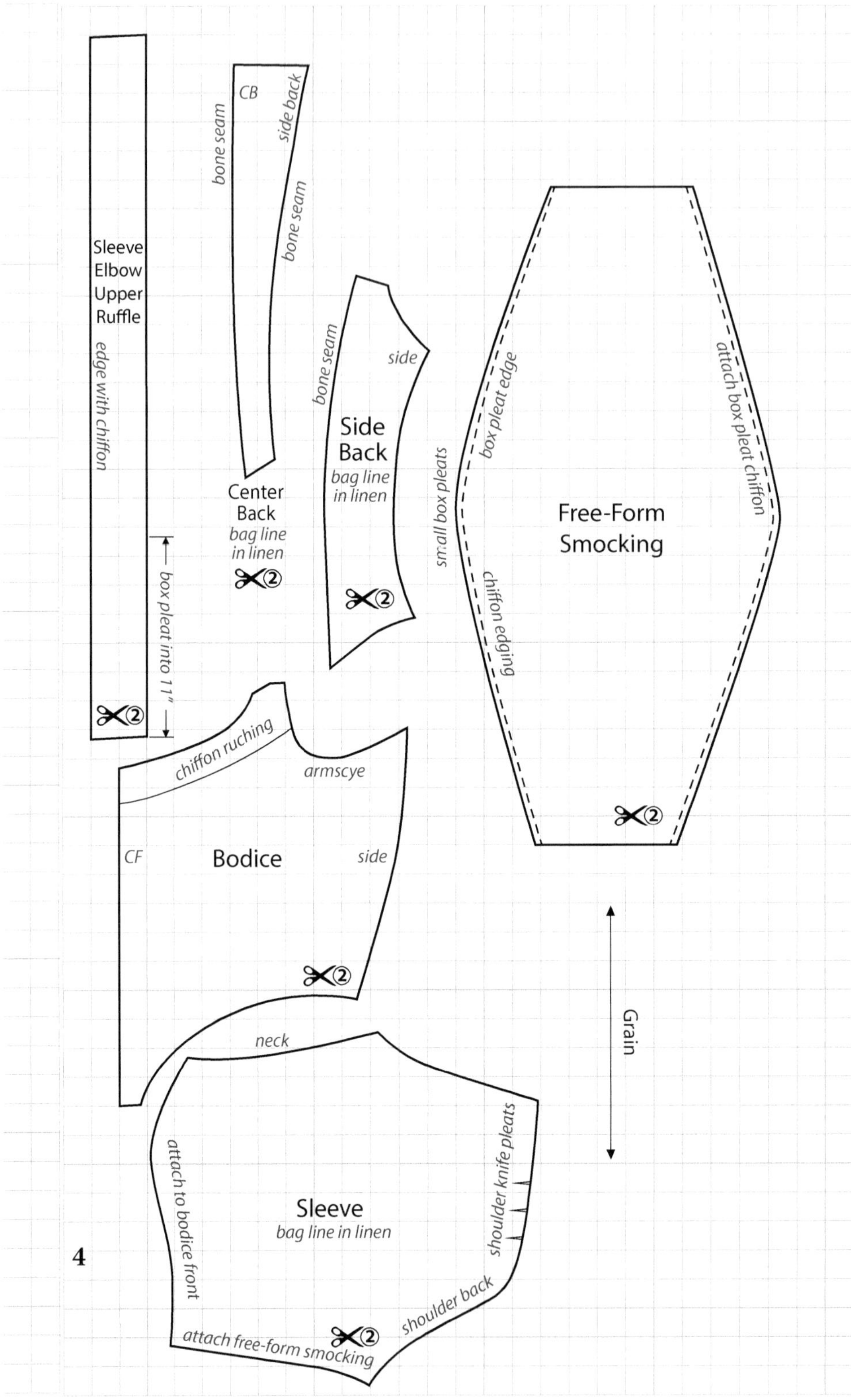
Sleeve
Elbow
Upper
Ruffle
edge with chiffon
box pleat into 11"
CB
bone seam
side back
bone seam
Center
Back
bag line
in linen
bone seam
side
Side
Back
bag line
in linen
small box pleats
box pleat edge
attach box pleat chiffon
Free-Form
Smocking
chiffon edging
chiffon ruching
armscye
CF
Bodice
side
Grain
neck
attach to bodice front
Sleeve
bag line in linen
shoulder knife pleats
shoulder back
attach free-form smocking
4

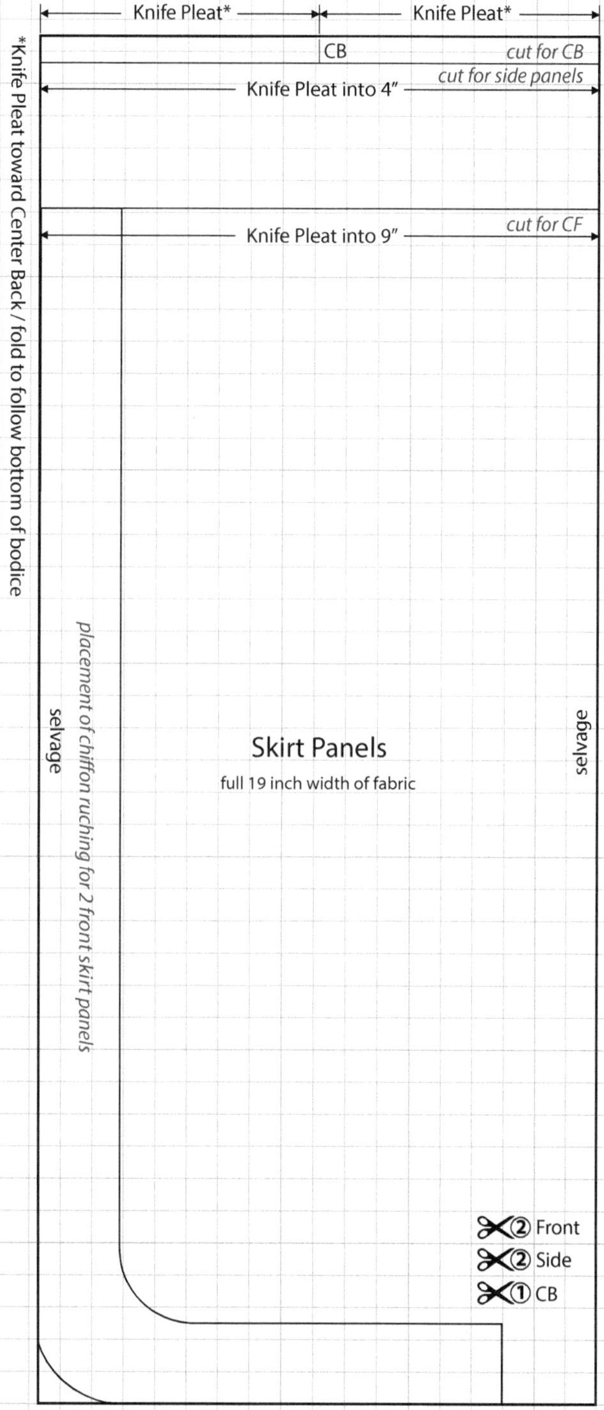
Knife Pleat*
Knife Pleat*
*Knife Pleat toward Center Back / fold to follow bottom of bodice
CB
cut for CB
cut for side panels
Knife Pleat into 4″
cut for CF
Knife Pleat into 9″
placement of chiffon ruching for 2 front skirt panels
selvage
selvage
Skirt Panels
full 19 inch width of fabric
② Front
② Side
① CB

1783

Striped Silk Polonaise

Back knife pleats at waist

Another contribution to the "country style" of the late 18th century is this lovely, blue- and cream-striped, silk polonaise. The popularity of striped fabrics spread in the 1770s. The gown was constructed in 1783, which was the same year that Marie Antoinette built her Little Hamlet. This gown was donated to the Hereford Museum in 1981.

This gown is a delightful example of "the country maiden." The engineering of this striped polonaise is different to that of the previous gown of eggshell blue grosgrain, which is held in place with two long loops of drawstring affixed to center back waist buttons. This gown is another style, swaged up with two sets of ties on the inside of the skirt. One tie is attached

Front shoulder

Inside

Lace cuff

Inside skirt ties

at the side back waist and the other is 14 inches down the skirt and slightly further forward (see image of the inside skirt ties). The skirt is made from seven 19-inch-wide skirt panels, which is the full width of the fabric selvage to selvage. The pocket opening is between panels 1 and 2 and 6 and 7. The pocket openings are finished by turning the selvage over twice, hiding a red line at the very edge of the selvage and sewing it with a tiny running stitch. The front panels are 36 inches in length and the center back is 42 inches in length. The front slopes to the center back.

The center front skirt panels are made shorter still in the front panel by 1½ inches and gradually lengthened as the hem moves to the back of the skirt. This was achieved by the front center skirt hem folded up the inch and a half and zeroing out at the original hem. The center skirt opening is flanked with two strips of scalloped, 2½-inch, ruched silk. The ruching is scalloped and pinked along the edges. One of the back skirt panels was carefully pieced together so that it matched the stripes at the top of the skirt and pleated into the waist. As this part of the skirt was intended to be caught up in the polonaise, the pieced together portion is almost indiscernible.

The bodice closes center front, with 11 eyelet holes on either side, allowing it to be laced up the front. This lacing is an homage to old-fashioned peasant styles. The sleeves are simply adorned at elbow-length and finished with a single ruffle of tan lace. The bodice and the sleeves are bag lined with cream linen.

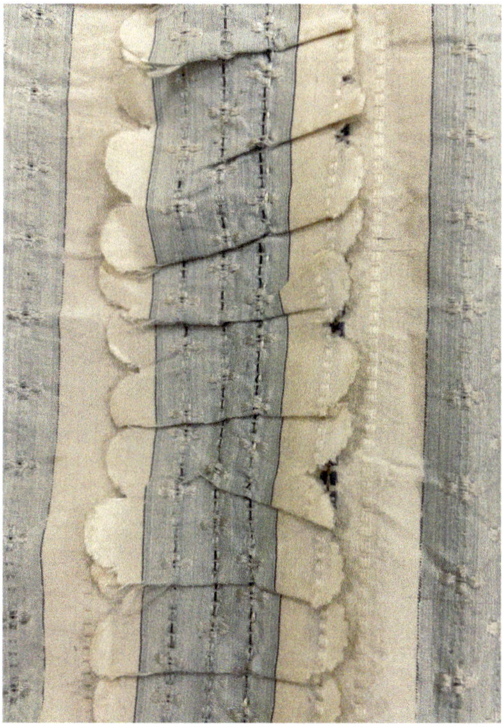

Scalloped ruching

Side

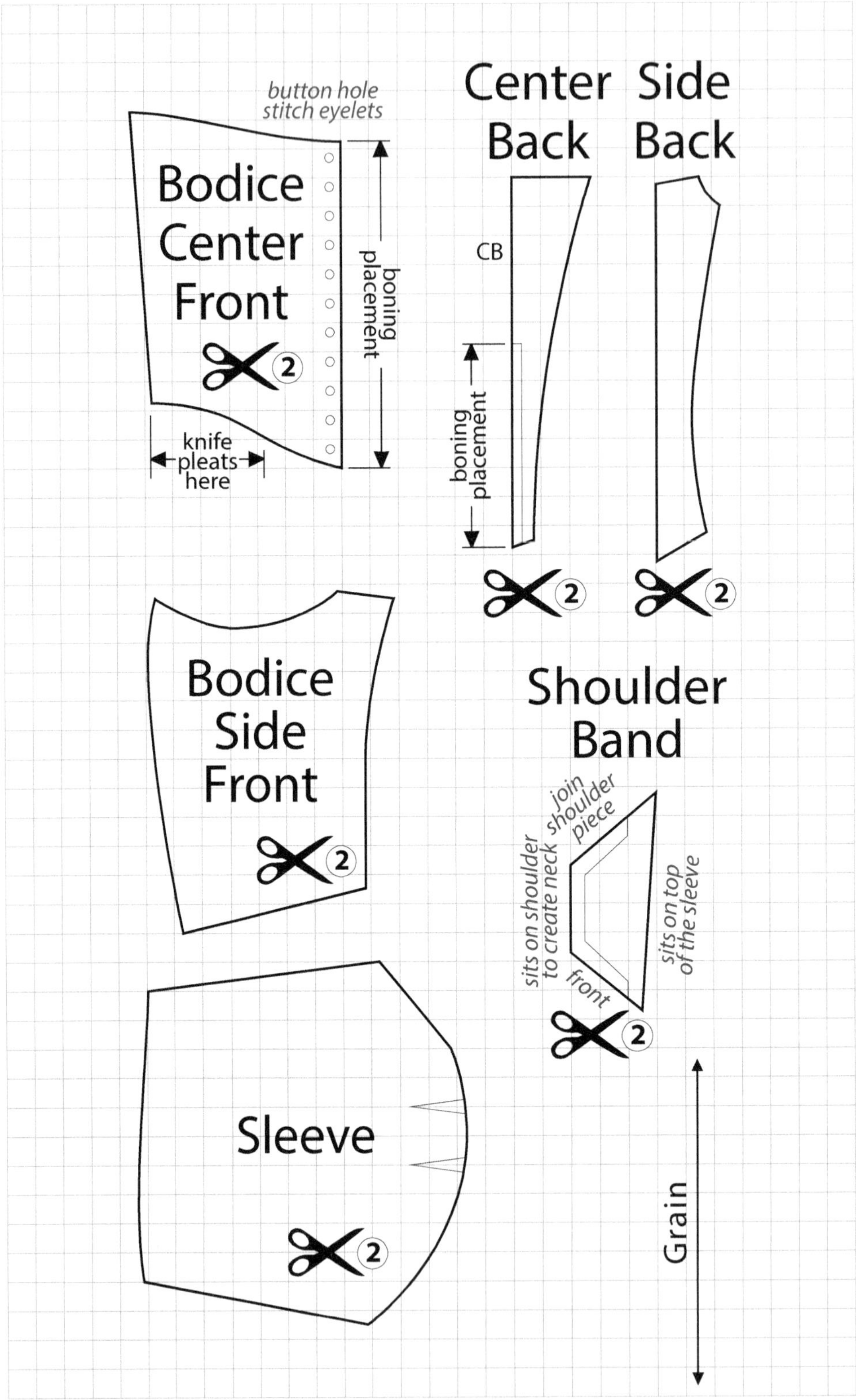
button hole stitch eyelets
Bodice Center Front
boning placement
knife pleats here
2
Center Back
CB
boning placement
2
Side Back
2
Bodice Side Front
2
Shoulder Band
join shoulder piece
sits on shoulder to create neck
sits on top of the sleeve
front
2
Sleeve
2
Grain

knife pleated into bodice
selvage
Skirt
full 19 inch width of fabric
selvage
7
gradual change in length
36″ length front panels
42″ length center back

1805

Striped Silk High Waist Dress

Center back bodice buttons

By 1805, dramatic and rapid changes in women's clothing had occurred. The British proclivity for country attire resulted in a change of style to a simple straight silhouette. An even more rapid change took place in France as a result of the social upheavals of the French Revolution.

The British continued to split their time between court and their country homes, unlike Napoleon's French counterparts, who remained at court. The British valued their time on their estates to pursue rural pastimes. This encouraged simpler forms of dress. Stays and petticoats were discarded. The full-skirted silhouette of the 18th century was replaced with a neoclassical ideal. At the same time, American style mirrored all things English, since many Americans still had ancestral ties with Britain.

Pocket slit

Bodice chevroned center front

Under collar

Trying to match skirt stripes

Even before the French Revolution, the French had an interest in all things British, including British freedoms. During the Reign of Terror, French clothing changed rapidly. Fashionable clothing became tantamount to a death sentence and fashion as an organized industry ceased to exist. Dresses with overt working-class affiliations were adopted. Jackets and skirts made from printed cotton became popular.

By 1805, this brown and tan silk gown emphasized a vertical silhouette. The column-like shape of the gown evokes the classical simplicity of an ancient Greece garment. This Regency style included the practical addition of long sleeves and a high neckline. The simple decoration appears in the form of the bodice center front chevron stripe pattern and strips of striped fabric that flank the edge of the collar and sleeve cuff.

This gown is made from tan and brown striped silk. The bottom of the short bodice finishes just under the bust. The center front seam is styled with a wide chevron. The striped fabric runs the length of the sleeves. The straight long sleeves would have covered most of the hand and is finished with a carefully cut cream stripe harvested from the fabric. The collar of the bodice has a fairly high stand and roll, with the collar tips spread out. The back of the collar sits high on the neck. The skirt is straight and is cut the same in the front and back. The skirt panels are 29 inches wide and are gathered at the waist with a casing and drawstring which ties in a bow.

The gown is closed at the center back with six ¾-inch brown buttons and buttonholes on a lapped placket. The top of the collar is closed with a hook and eye. The shoulder seams sit back on the bodice from the side back of the neck to the center of the back of the armscyes.

The person who made this gown had their heart set on a vertical striped dress. If you look closely at the photograph you can see that the skirt of the dress is carefully pieced together across the hip to achieve the long bust-to-hem stripes. It was constructed from a 32-inch-wide striped fabric.

Inside bodice

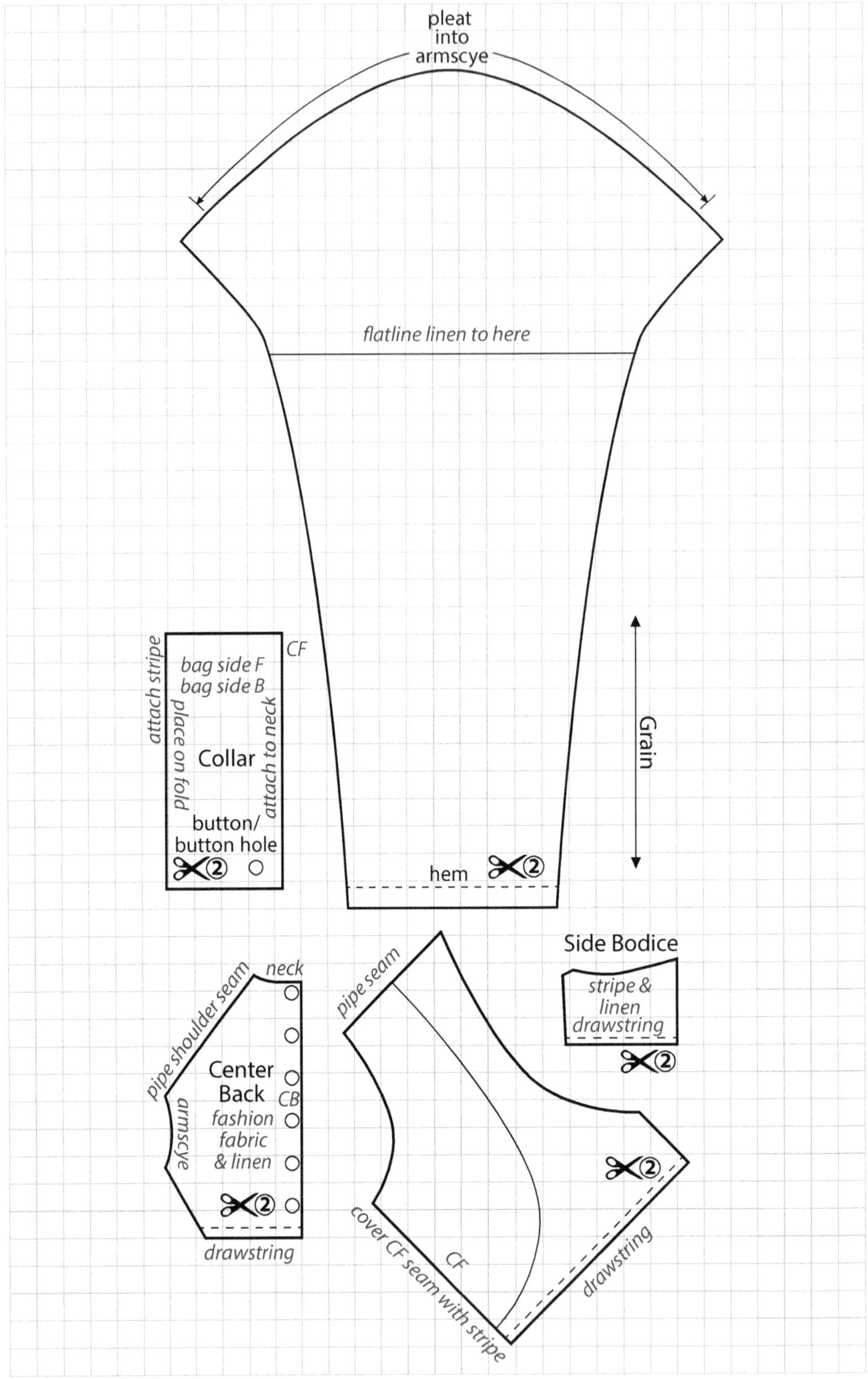
pleat
into
armscye
flatline linen to here
Grain
hem
2
CF
attach stripe
bag side F
bag side B
place on fold
Collar
attach to neck
button/
button hole
2
neck
pipe shoulder seam
Center
Back
CB
fashion
fabric
& linen
armscye
2
drawstring
pipe seam
cover CF seam with stripe
CF
drawstring
2
Side Bodice
stripe &
linen
drawstring
2

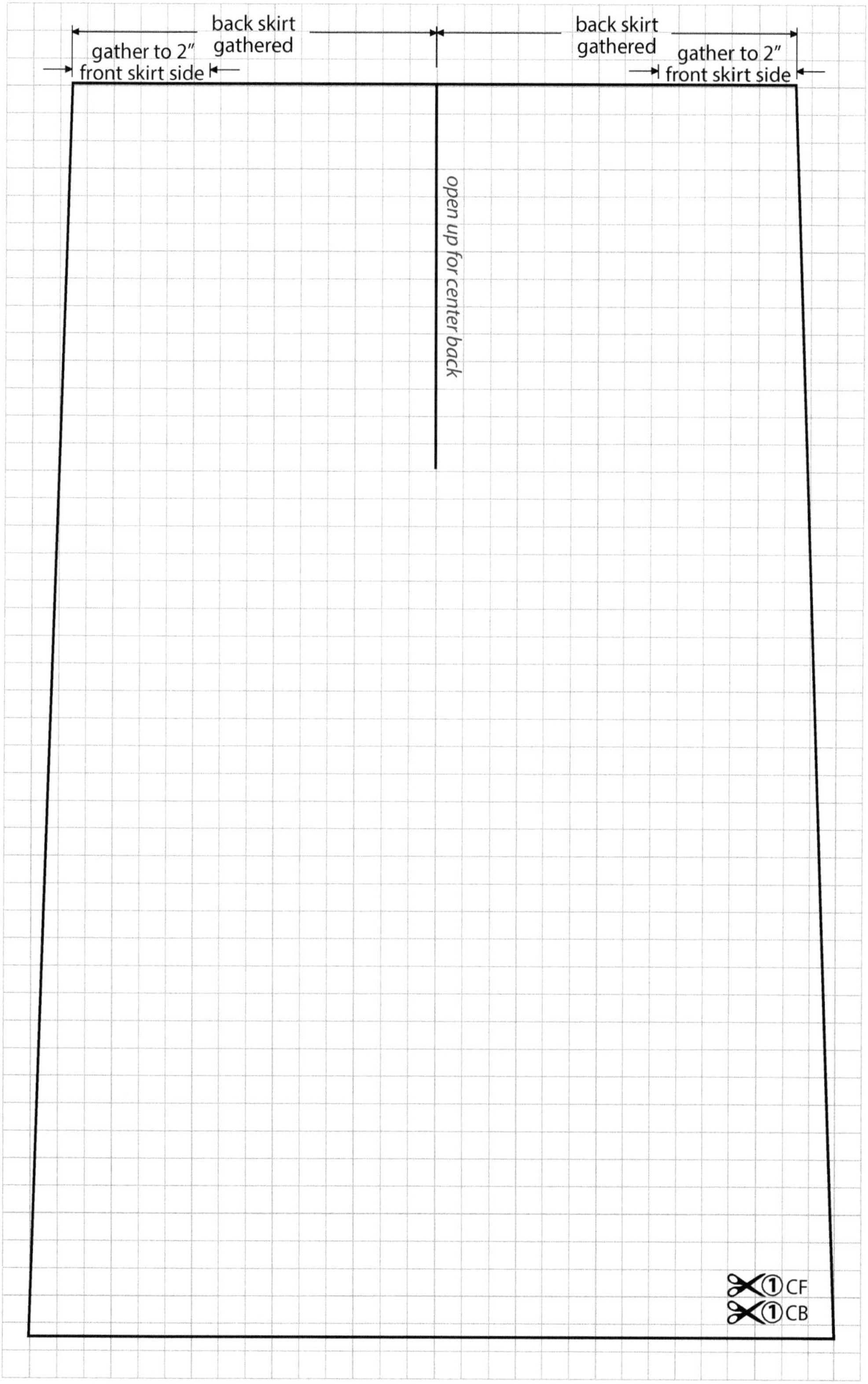
back skirt
gathered
gather to 2″
front skirt side
back skirt
gathered
gather to 2″
front skirt side
open up for center back
1 CF
1 CB

1810

Cotton Lawn High Waist Dress with Appliques

Radial gathers in front bodice

This high-waisted cotton lawn gown reflects many influences. In the late 18th century, a dress for a young girl might be a white muslin. The shape and style of this 1810 gown are much the same as a little girl's dresses. Also, the lines of classical antiquity are apparent. The popularity of white cotton, like the white marble from which both classical and neo-classical statues were made, coincided with a growing passion for the use of white in women's clothing. This also went hand in hand with the Neoclassical movement. Another revolution of the late 18th century was in the production of cotton.

Simplicity rather than ostentation became the new fashion of choice. From 1800, white muslin became a preferred fabric that adorned the feminine form for nearly 20 years.

Gathers in puff sleeve

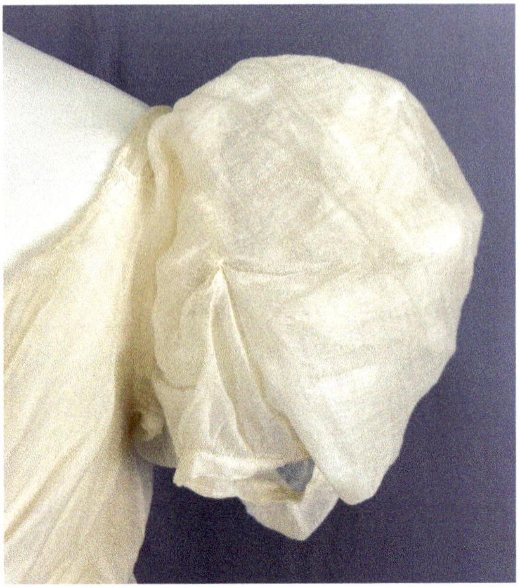

Puff sleeve

Applique

Eli Whitney's cotton gin transformed the production of cotton in the southern United States. After its invention, the yield of raw cotton doubled each decade after 1800. Raw cotton was sent to British mills. This resulted in a supply of cheap cotton that was functional, practical, and more launderable, and was also much more sanitary. This created public health benefits wherever it was adopted.

This gown has a beautiful floral border from India. It showcases the skills and designs of another sophisticated cotton industry. Unfortunately, the cotton gin also made American slavery much more profitable in the years before the American Civil War.

This dress is finished along the hem with a foot-deep applique of assorted blooms. The bottom of the applique is a run of joined scalloped flowers. It was likely that the panel of the overskirt was purchased in one piece and imported from India. The skirt is gathered across the back of the bodice. The front of the garment is shaped at the side with a wedge of the lawn cut out and finished with a tiny seam going to, but not through, the bottom embroidery. The tiny seams where the wedges were removed are the placement for pocket slits. These sit at the hip. In my pattern the skirt front reflects the finished shape of the skirt front after the wedge was taken out, which was used for the cotton underskirt.

The bodice neckline is square, with a tiny drawstring ruffle. The short puff sleeves have a front and side cluster of gathers. The gathers give the puff sleeve a bit of its own thrust as well as a control twill tape that holds the sleeve gathers in place. The sleeve cuff is finished with a delicate bias edge. The bodice is shaped with gathers that start center front and radiate to just under the bust. The high waist has a 2½-inch solid ribbon edge sewn along the top of the ribbon reinforcing the top of the skirt.

Grecian hairstyles were adopted to top a gown like this one, once again embracing the Neoclassical ideal. A less substantial foundation garment replaced the 18th-century stays and petticoat. Undergarments, in general, were reduced to a minimum.

Control twill tape to hold gather in place

Applique hem shaped with large tucks

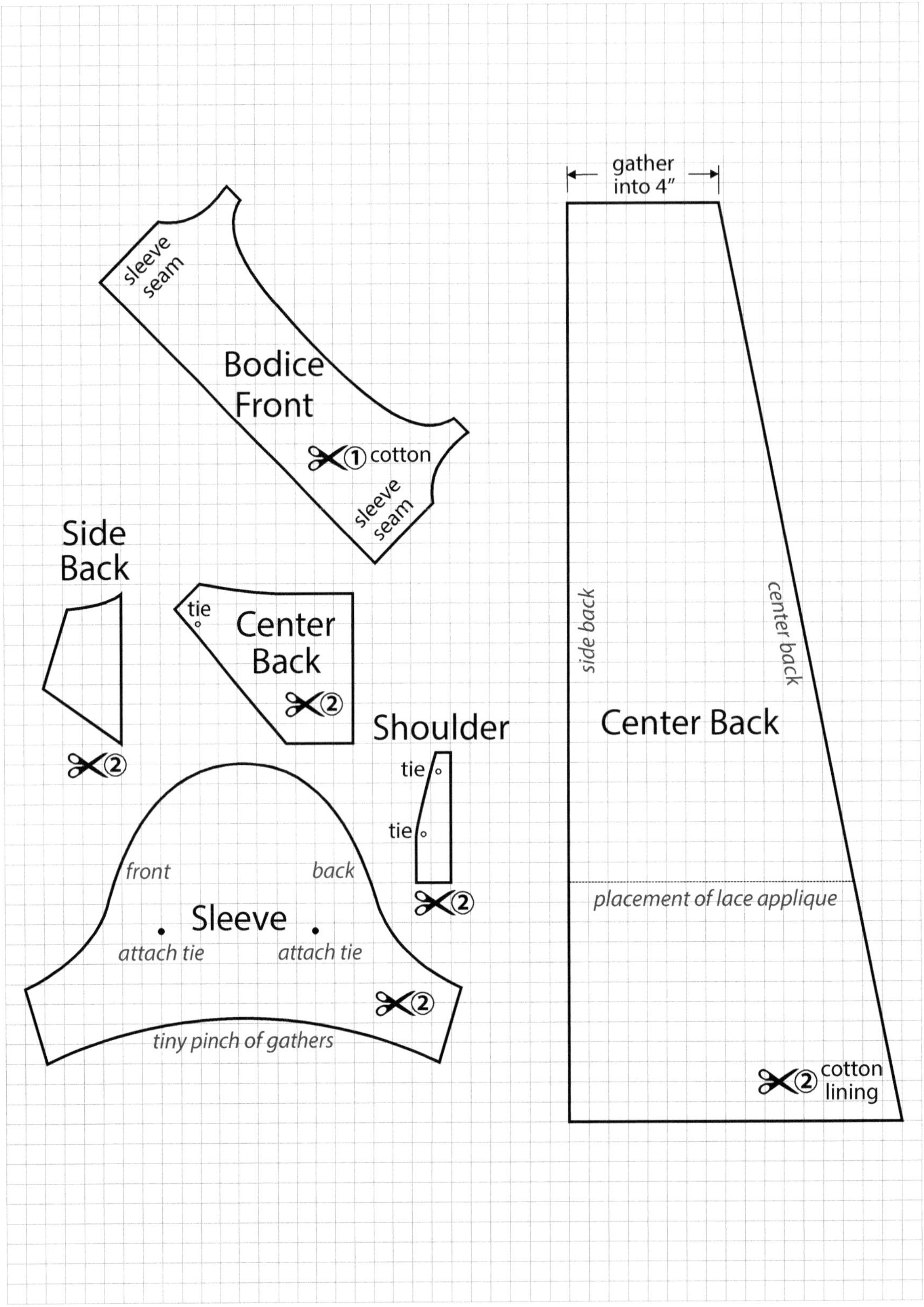
gather into 4″
sleeve seam
Bodice Front
1 cotton
sleeve seam
Side Back
2
tie
Center Back
2
Shoulder
tie
tie
2
side back
center back
Center Back
placement of lace applique
2 cotton lining
front
back
Sleeve
attach tie
attach tie
2
tiny pinch of gathers

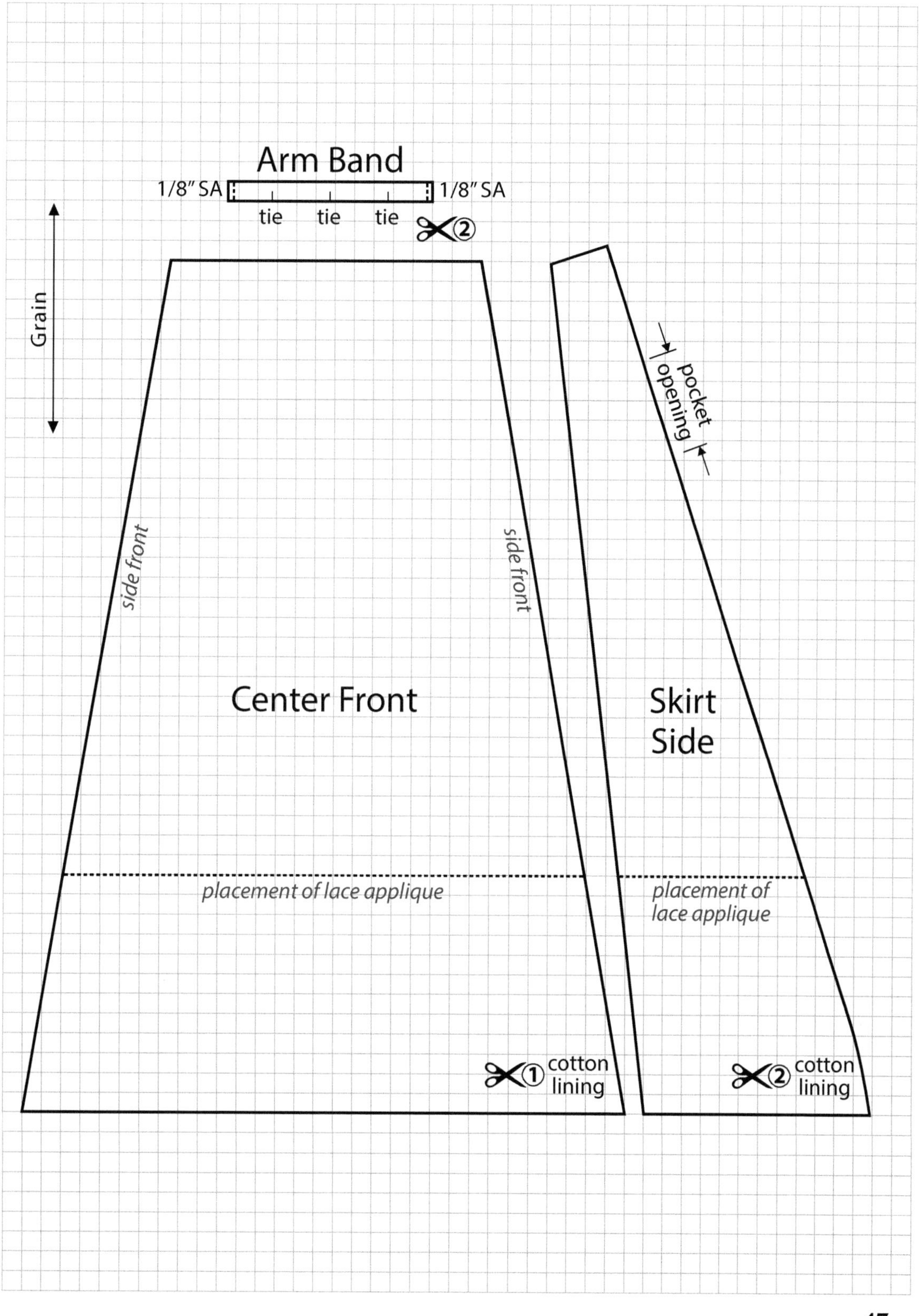
Arm Band
1/8″ SA
1/8″ SA
tie
tie
tie
2
Grain
side front
side front
Center Front
placement of lace applique
1
cotton lining
pocket opening
Skirt Side
placement of lace applique
2
cotton lining

1825

Floral Print Cotton Gauze Dress

Cotton print with lavender irises

Bodice sleeve cap, upper puff, bias ruffle

In 1793 the Eli Whitney cotton gin greatly reduced the expense of preparing cotton for spinning and weaving. Cotton became more profitable and affordable. Improved sanitation and public health were unexpected benefits of this easily laundered fabric. Cotton was a cheaper, healthier, quality fabric.

American slavery had begun to fade prior to the early 1790s. Whitney's cotton gin fueled a cotton mania but also had the unfortunate consequence of African slavery. Lives changed for all who worked along the cotton chain – planting, harvesting, cleaning, spinning, weaving, dyeing, and printing. Textile factories in the early Industrial Revolution worked adults and children 70 hours a week, sometimes more. In Britain, there was a huge demand for cotton mill workers that was rapidly increasing. By 1815, cotton had become a standard part of men's and women's wardrobes.

The Romantic style lines of this 1825 dress were part of the Romantic

Control strip of piped bias for center front bust gathers

reaction to the inhumanity of the Industrial Revolution. The movement emphasized intense emotion as a source of aesthetic expression. Medieval and Renaissance elements were desirable effects in art and narrative. Romantic artistic expression is seen in both the full upper sleeve puffs and the return of a fuller style skirt, both reminiscent of the Renaissance.

This gown is made from a printed cotton gauze. The print is made from a process called pin ground, named for the small dots in the background. It was first printed with the lavender and black. Another run block printed the green. The yellow and red may have been "pencilled" (painted in) by hand, usually by females. By 1825, delicate floral prints on light backgrounds had become increasingly popular. The white fabric has bright lavender and green irises outlined in black.

The gown is cut with a slightly lower waist from the previous period. The bodice front is gathered at the center front from the neckline to under the bust. The bodice is flatlined with lightweight linen. The center back unlined fabric is gathered into the neckline and waistband. The neckline is bound with a small self-bias band. The puff sleeve sits slightly off the shoulder and is gathered into the armscye and the narrow lower sleeve. A bias ruffle separates the shoulder puff and the lower sleeve. The gathers at the armscye, the off-the-shoulder panel, the lower sleeve and the center bodice gathers are all piped with bias self-piping. On the inside of the upper sleeve puff, top and bottom, are a set of control ties that help maintain the shape of the puff.

The skirt is made from four panels of the 34-inch-wide fabric with the selvage running waist to hem. A 6-inch linen strip faces the lower edge of the hem giving it gentle support. The center back waist is closed with two sets of hooks and eyes on the waistband. The side seams have 11-inch pocket slits that sit 1½ inches down from the waistband.

Pocket slits

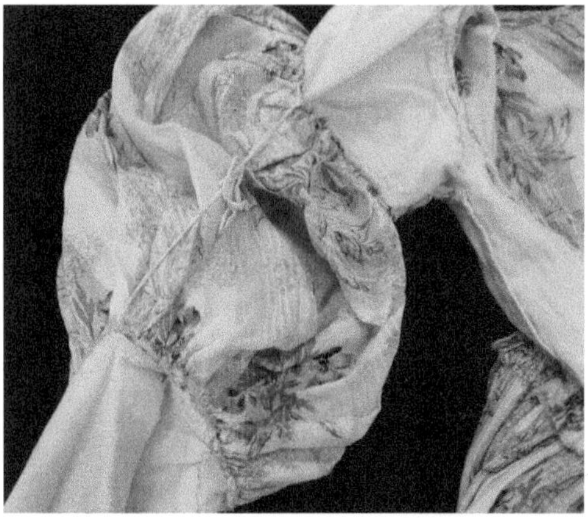

Control ties

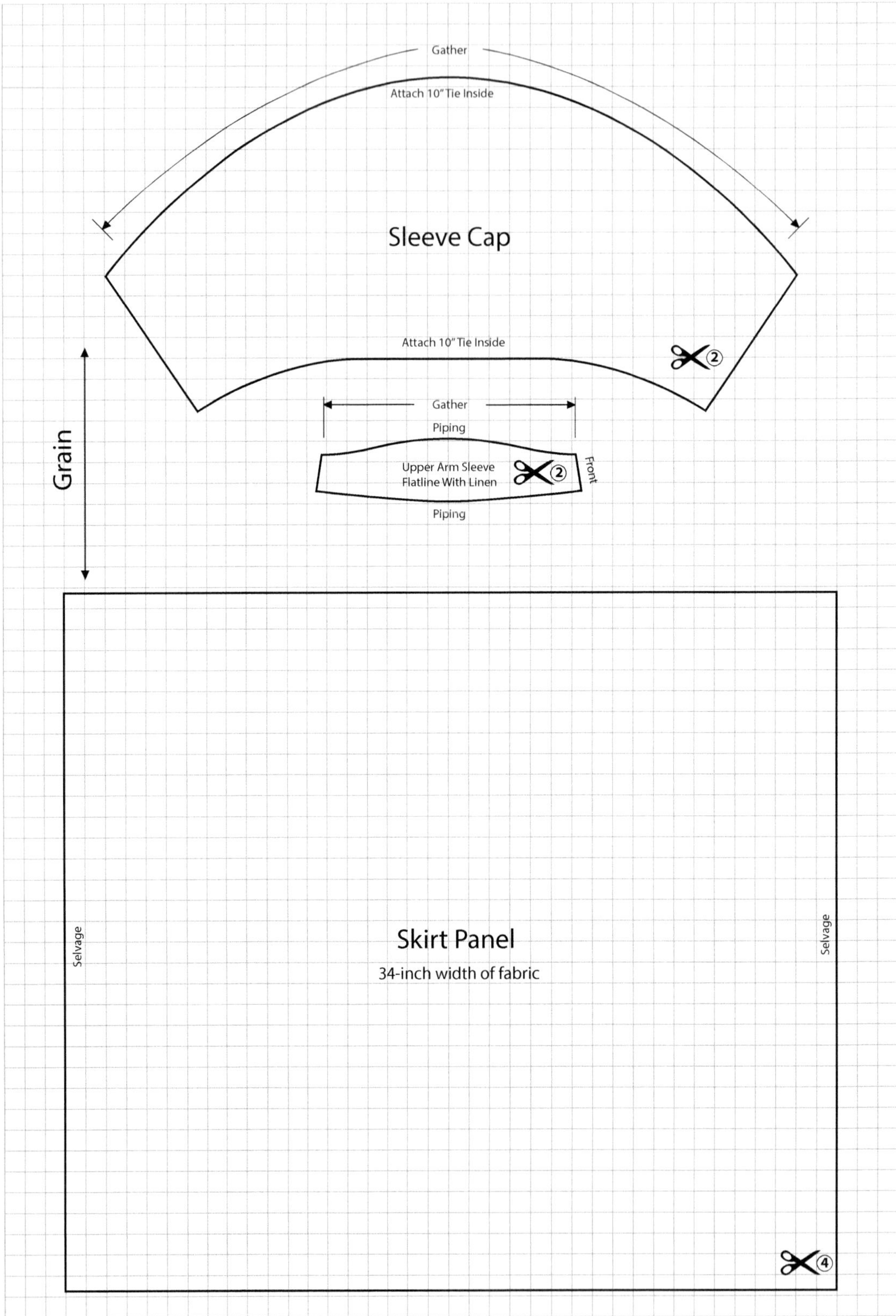
Gather
Attach 10" Tie Inside
Sleeve Cap
Attach 10" Tie Inside
2
Gather
Piping
Upper Arm Sleeve
Flatline With Linen
2
Front
Piping
Grain
Selvage
Skirt Panel
34-inch width of fabric
Selvage
4

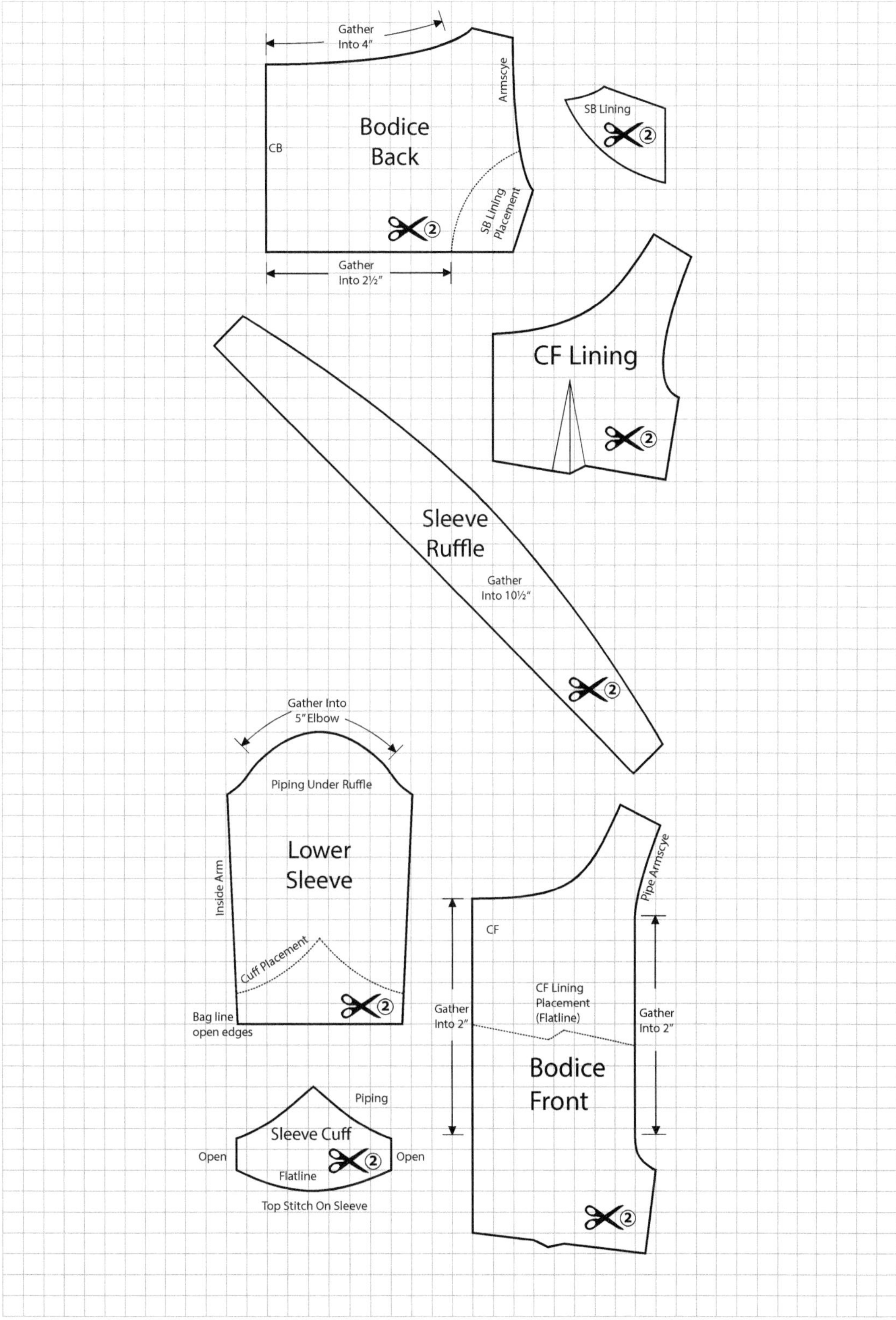
Gather
Into 4″
Armscye
Bodice
Back
CB
SB Lining
Placement
Gather
Into 2½″
SB Lining
CF Lining
Sleeve
Ruffle
Gather
Into 10½″
Gather Into
5″ Elbow
Piping Under Ruffle
Lower
Sleeve
Inside Arm
Cuff Placement
Bag line
open edges
Pipe Armscye
CF
CF Lining
Placement
(Flatline)
Gather
Into 2″
Gather
Into 2″
Bodice
Front
Piping
Sleeve Cuff
Open
Open
Flatline
Top Stitch On Sleeve

1834

– – Striped Cotton Print Wedding Dress – –

The early 19th century ushered in the age of steam. By 1831 the first commercial steam railway line was built from Liverpool to Manchester. It was built to transport textile products from the mills in Manchester (nicknamed Cottonopolis) to the port at Liverpool. By 1830 the steam use of power was extended to textile power looms and in 1838 the Great Western Steamship Company crossed the Atlantic from Bristol to New York in 15 days.

The process of printed fabric also advanced. Roller printing became more sophisticated, which allowed for intricate patterns and vivid colors. Early machines could print only one color but designs were often enhanced by adding additional colors with the older block printing method. The fabric in this dress has an active, abstract pattern with imaginary vegetation of Romantic originality. Stripes are created with a sky-blue background, which is shot through with organic white lines and tiny black crescents. Between the stripes are white areas covered with little tan circles and dots and unusual flowers of tan, red, and green with serpentine black lines trailing throughout.

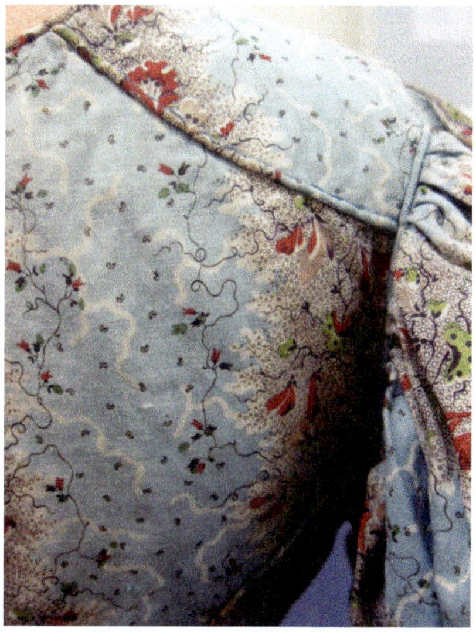

Bodice back, shoulder seam

Inside shoulder cap seam

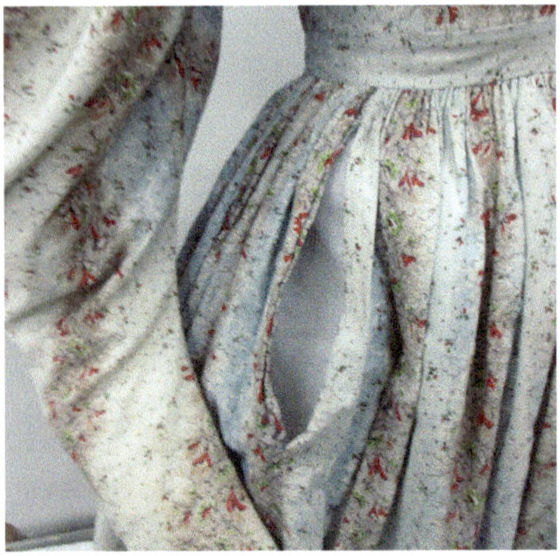

Skirt pocket opening

Faced bodice and skirt hem

Technological advances in the production of textiles made trim and laces much more accessible. Handmade lace became a thing of the past and it could be manufactured in both narrow and wide widths. By 1834, this dress, with its unadorned neckline, could be worn with a variety of lace collars, pelerines or chemisettes.

Romantic overtones can also be seen in the exaggerated silhouette of the dress. With outsized shoulders the style continues as seen with the 63-inch width of the sleeve cap. This style of dress embraces large sleeves, a popular style of the period, but as a practical dress, it avoids other excesses.

This cotton print dress was made by Hereford seamstress, Mary Bufton. This was Mary's wedding dress. Before marriage she was a smock maker. Heavy linen or wool smocks were worn by farmers, dairymen, and shepherds to protect their clothes. Mary was well established as an accomplished seamstress before marriage to a local farmer. This dress was beautifully constructed with the careful even stitches of a master seamstress planning her upcoming marriage. It is a stunning example of early 19th century craftmanship in the Hereford collection.

While working on this dress I discovered some very clever clothing construction practices. The striped fabric is carefully cut so the center front of the bodice creates a chevron which emphasizes the width of the cap of the sleeves. The sleeves are cut on the bias of the 26-inch-wide fabric, so the bottoms of the sleeves fit quite snug from elbow to wrist. To accommodate the full cap of the bias-cut sleeve, a seam is hidden in the gathers of the sleeve cap. This piece was harvested from the curve of the elbow to the wrist of the sleeve.

Mary chose a colorful print that could be used for many occasions. This exotic collection of real and imaginary organic shapes, as well as vines and flowers, defines the stripes on this fabric. The fabric is 26 inches wide. This skirt had once been about two inches shorter. In the lower area of the skirt you can see where a grow tuck had once been. Shorter skirts were indeed more popular in the early 1830s. Perhaps it was Mary herself who wore the dress shorter.

The two-piece front bodice is cut on the diagonal. Each bodice seam, including the center front, the armscyes, the shoulder and side back, are piped with self-piping. The neckline is also finished with self-bias tape. The bias-cut sleeves allow the stripes to add another playful angle to the dress.

The full 26-inch width of fabric was used in each skirt panel. The selvage edges can be seen on either side of the four skirt panel lengths. The skirt is faced with 8 inches of muslin, which gives a slight thrust to the bottom of the skirt.

Mary's careful stitching

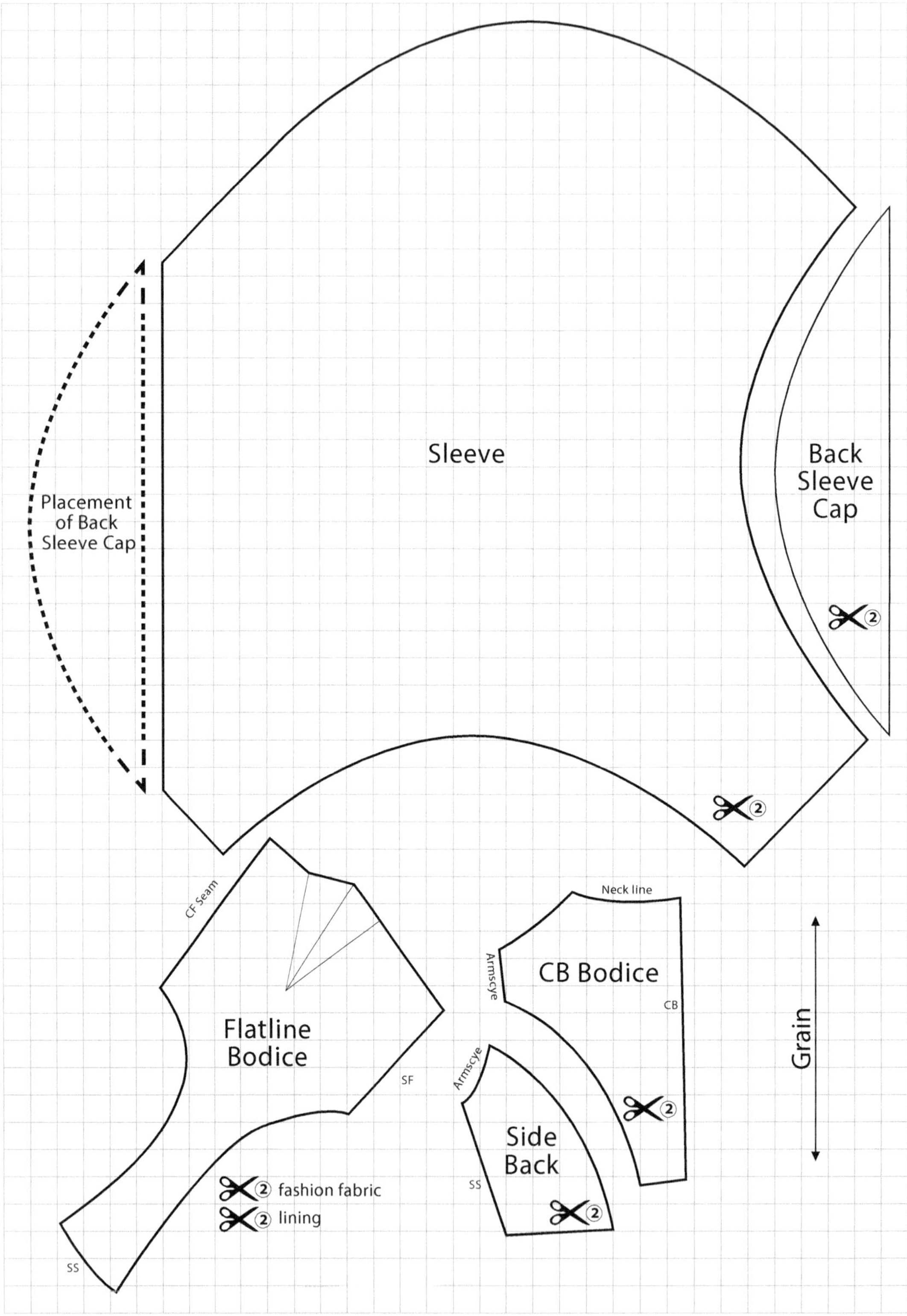
Sleeve
Placement of Back Sleeve Cap
Back Sleeve Cap
2
2
CF Seam
Flatline Bodice
SF
SS
2 fashion fabric
2 lining
Neck line
Armscye
CB Bodice
CB
2
Armscye
Side Back
SS
2
Grain

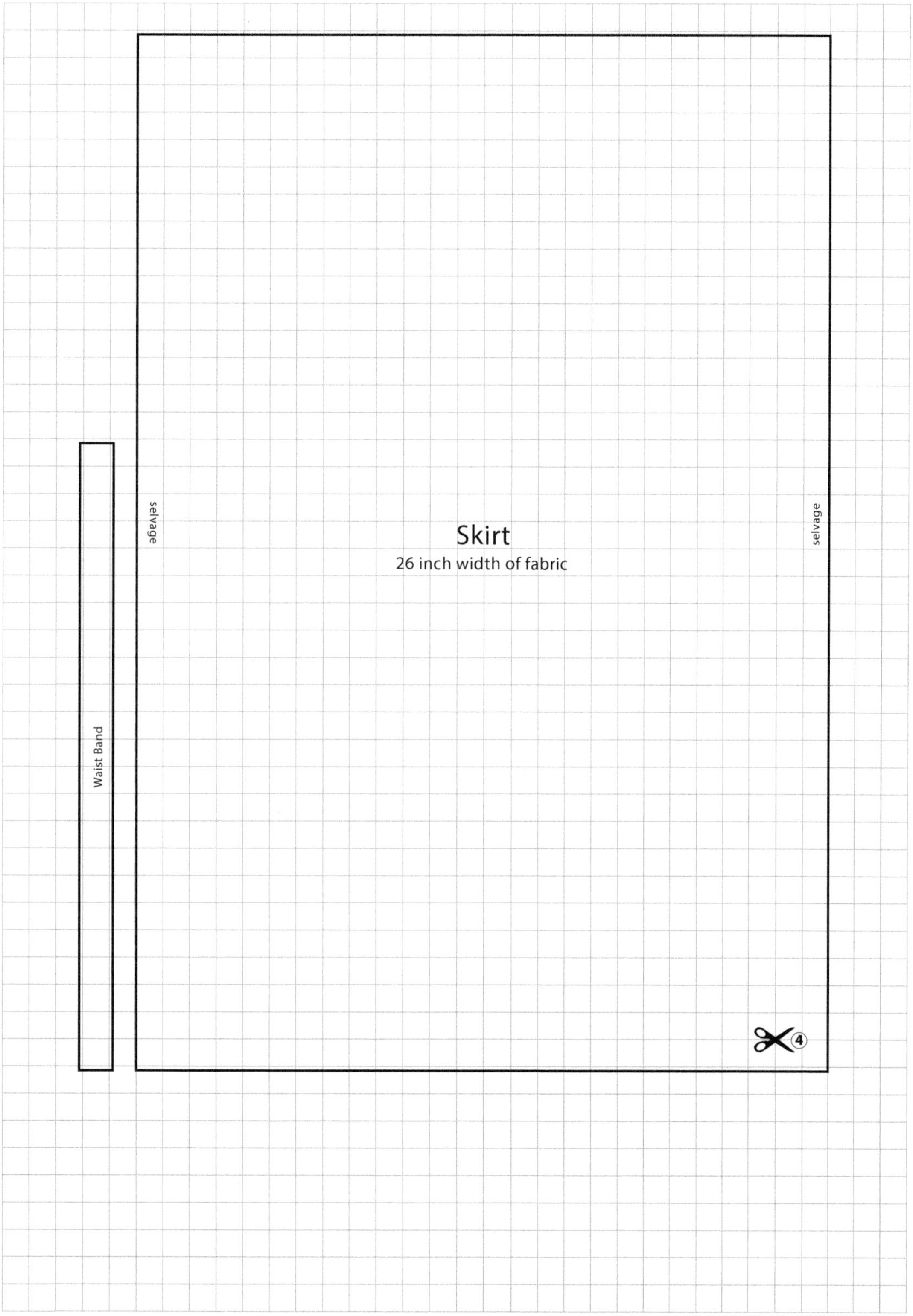
Skirt
26 inch width of fabric
selvage
selvage
Waist Band
4

1850

Striped Wool Printed Dress

On May 1, 1851, Queen Victoria opened the *Great Exhibition of the Works of Industry of all Nations* at the Crystal Palace in London. It is referred to as the *Crystal Palace Exhibition*, after the glass and iron structure in which it was housed. It was a spectacular celebration of modern industrial technology and design. It was also the first international trade exhibition. It was an expo for manufacturers to display their technical and artistic achievements.

The American exhibit included Elias Howe's sewing machine. The sewing machine became the first complex household appliance to find a national market in both America and the British Empire. Howe's company was later taken over by the more familiar American entrepreneur and businessman, Isaac Singer. The intricate layers of this dress would have benefited from the sewing machine, but this dress was made entirely by hand.

By the 1850s men's clothing took on a somber, utilitarian mode with dark colors which easily hid the industrial soot that filled urban air. Women's clothing, on the other hand, became decorative, eye-catching and inconvenient. The multiple layers of petticoats filled her dress to a large bell shape, which also served as a display of family wealth.

Technical improvements in textiles, combined with the popularity of historical

Side view of bodice

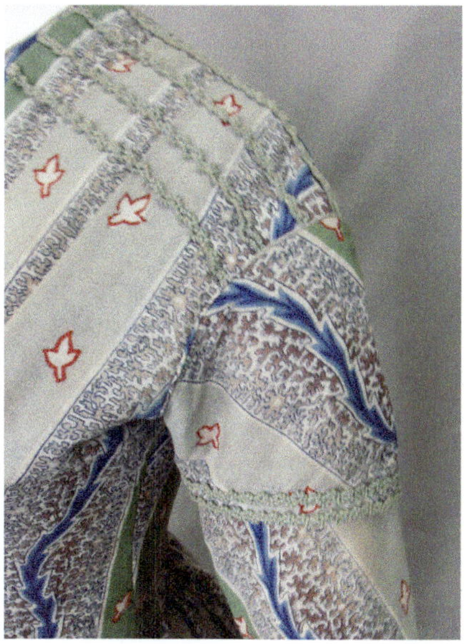

Trim on shoulder and shoulder cap

Inside muslin-lined bodice-skirt panels folded along bodice bottom

Hook and eyelet center back closure

revival styles, produced some spectacular fabrics for both dress and furnishings. This applied to all types of textiles, including the printed wool of this gown. The print has an elaborate pattern combined with unusual colors including leaf green, tan, electric blue, cream, and scarlet. This day dress looks primarily green striped but includes a variation of exotic patterns.

With mounting British conflicts in the Far East, military motifs once again are included as a decorative element. An almost hidden military motif appears on the front of the bodice and center front skirt panel. Strips of green gimp, finished with green buttons, flank the center front of the bodice and the center front of the skirt panel. Because the pattern of the gown is so busy, the military motif is almost lost in the fabric. When I made a mockup of this dress in white, the military motif became quite apparent.
The bodice is attached to the skirt and it has three knife pleats facing the center front. The bodice is flatlined with muslin. The simple neckline sits at the base of the neck. The skirt/bodice seam, shoulder cap, and neckline seam are finished in self-piping. Four lines of green gimp run across the shoulder-

to-waist pleats and six double rows of gimp (edged with two green buttons each) flank the center of the bodice from under the bust to the waist.

At the top of the sleeve is a 4-inch bias cap that sits out over the top of the sleeve. It is edged with two rows of the gimp. The narrow sleeve is finished with four rows of ½-inch overlapped self-bias fabric chevrons, slightly curved up at the front of the sleeve cuff. They are dotted with three decorative green buttons. The sleeves are flatlined with muslin.

The fullness of the skirt is an early example of the trend of extravagant growth in the shape of women's skirts. It is made from six 25-inch-wide skirt panels. The skirt is flatlined with a light weight crinoline. The bottom of the skirt is faced with muslin and has a center front decorative panel. The narrow panel is gored and cut on the bias, emphasizing the stripes. The gored piece is outlined with the same green gimp and it is attached to the skirt with 15 centered green buttons. A strip of green horsehair braid is sewn to extend half an inch beyond the edge of the hem to protect the hem bottom from wear.

Center front decorative skirt panel

Inside muslin-lined bodice

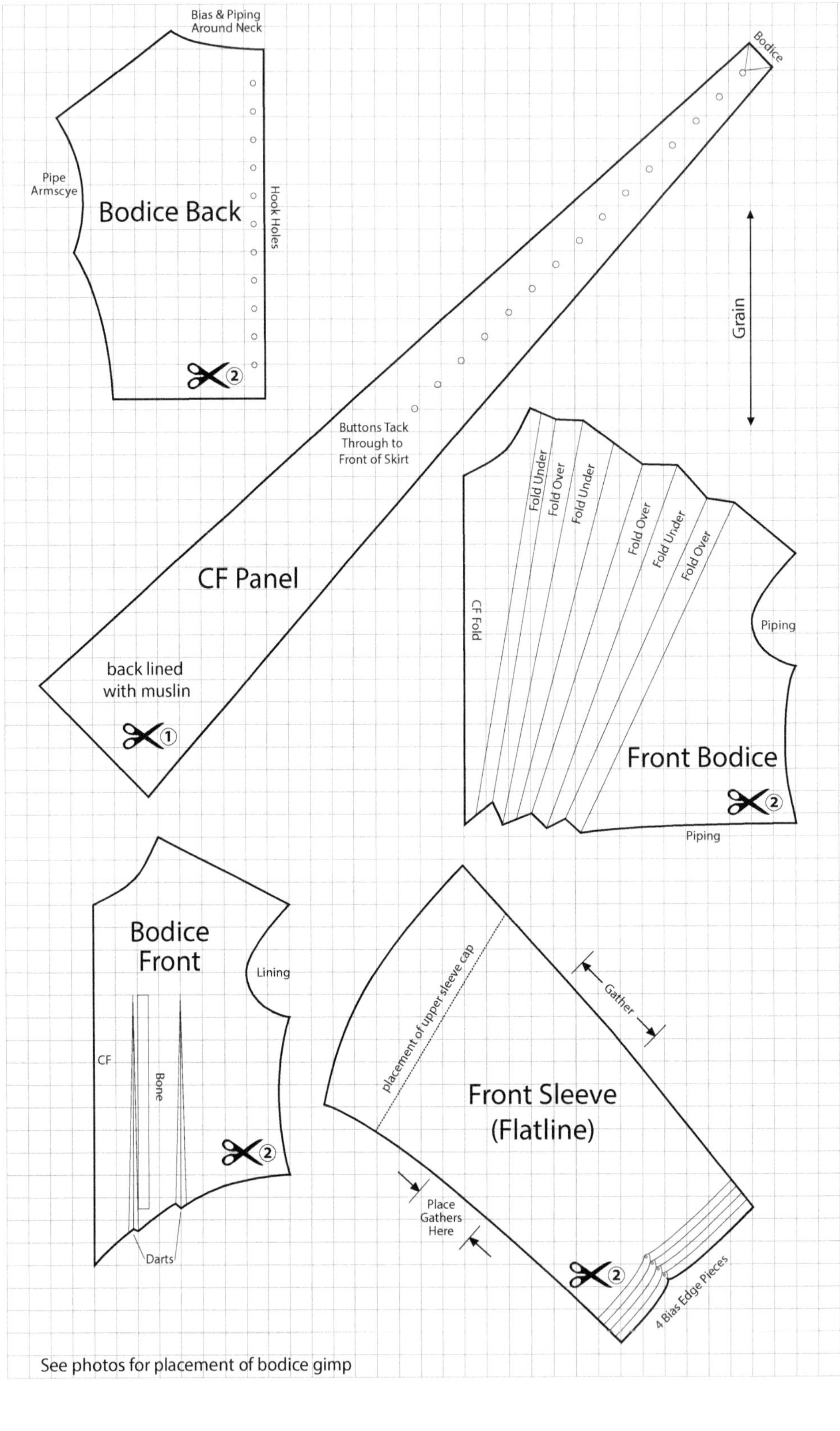

See photos for placement of bodice gimp

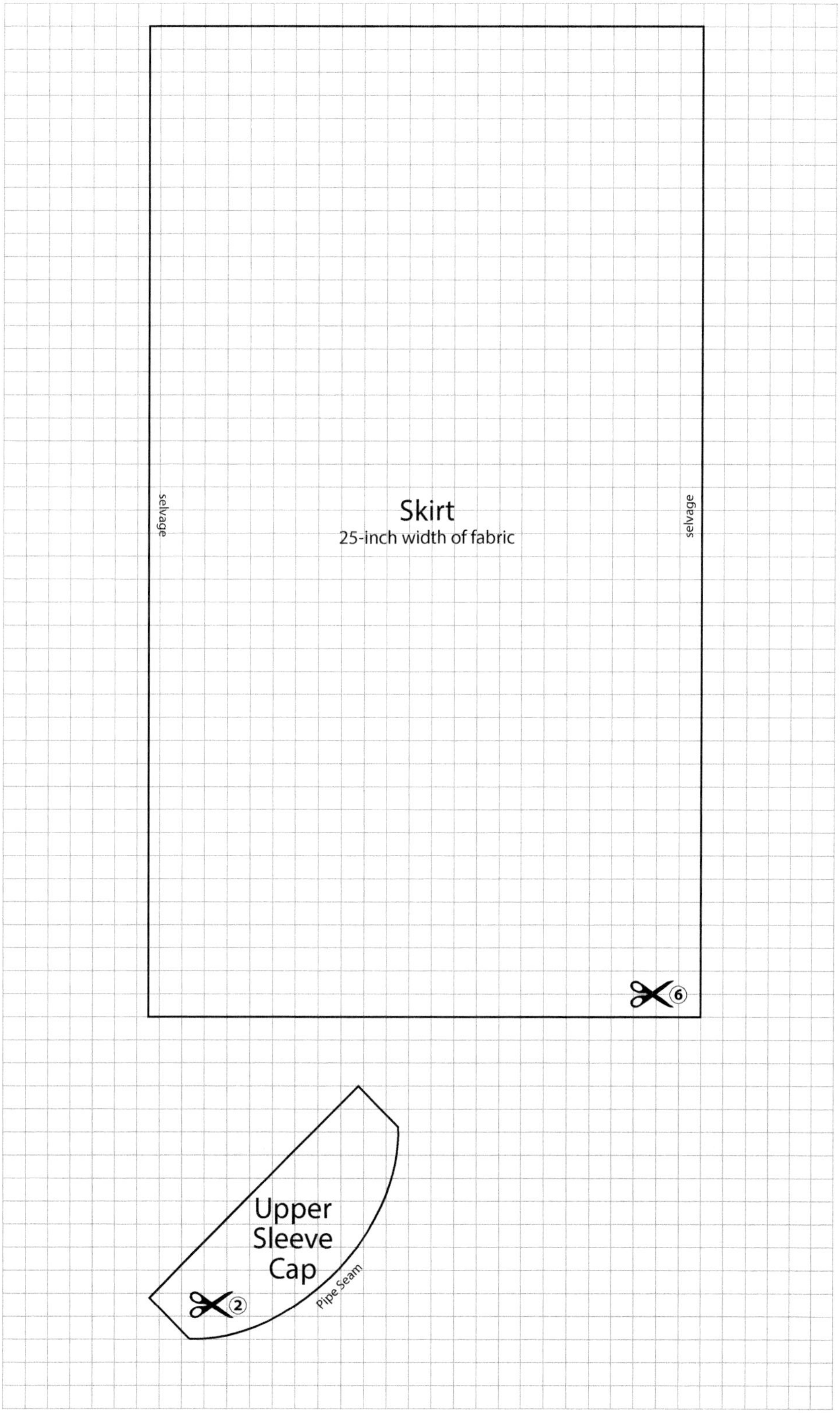

selvage
Skirt
25-inch width of fabric
selvage
6
Upper
Sleeve
Cap
2
Pipe Seam

1865

Silk Suit with Military Trim

By 1865, the British Empire had grown to include territories on every continent, inspiring the phrase "the empire on which the sun never set." Industrial England was in a great economic boom. France concluded a bloody civil war and proceeded to return as the city of indulgences and extravagances. The United States had been united by the transcontinental railroad. Westward expansion by rail, boat, and covered wagon introduced new immigrants to American cities from coast to coast.

England and the U.S. were entrenched in the moralistic tone of the Victorian era. The era of the agrarian past was coming to an end and left many with a sense of loss. The nostalgic past was being replaced by self-observation, clinical analyses and the scientific study of people. Darwin and his theory of evolution contributed to this mindset. Many people maintained their passion for Romanticism, which was transformed into excessive materialism. The forward-thinking elite found themselves embroiled in realism and social change. Any well-appointed front parlor was overstuffed and excessively ornamented.

The Industrial Revolution continued its rapid expansion. The need for workers to keep up with consumers' hunger for conspicuous consumption was enormous. During the mid-19th century, there was a large increase in both population and per capita income.

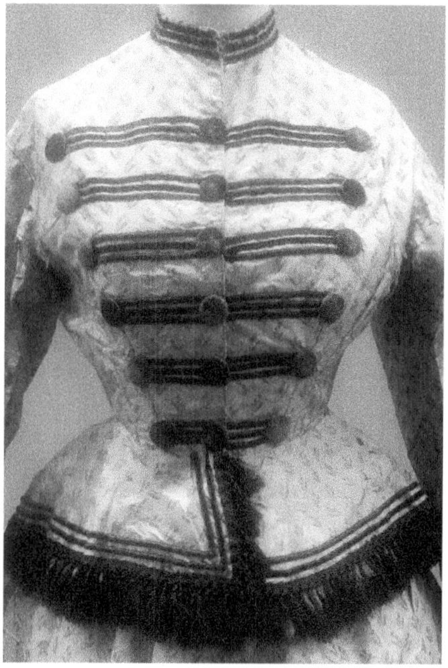

Jacket detail

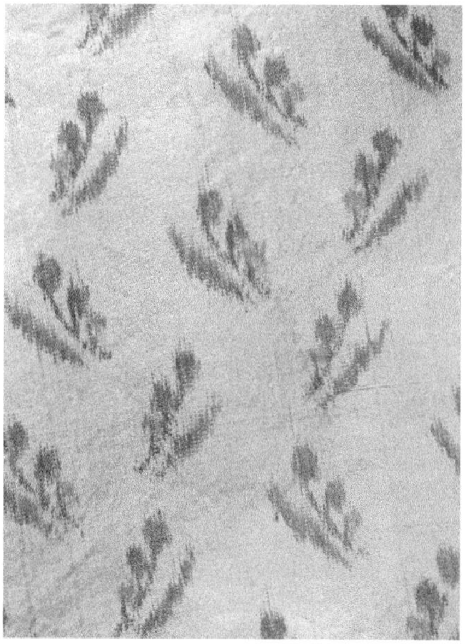

Fabric detail

Front

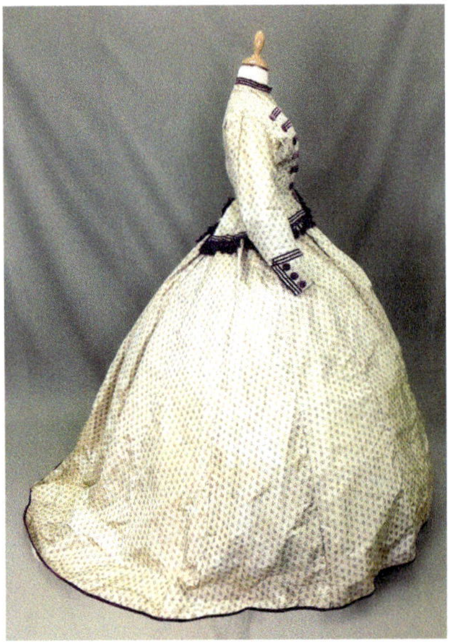

Side

By 1865, unprecedented prosperity fueled one of the first haute couture houses, the House of Worth. British born Charles Fredrick Worth established it in Paris in 1858. The House of Worth salon attracted European royalty. Wherever royalty led the nouveau riche society followed. Worth won the French aristocrat, Empress Eugenie, as a client and he supplied wealthy patrons on both sides of the Atlantic. Worth's aggressive self-promotion earned him the title "father of haute couture." He was the first to use live models to promote his garments to clients and the first to sew branded labels into his clothing. A visit to The House of Worth became a societal meeting point. Much of Worth's influence set the standard for other haute couture houses.

By the mid-1850s heavy petticoats were replaced with steel, whale bone or wicker cage hoop. By 1860, the size of the hoop skirt grew to extremes and by 1865 began to be pulled flat in front, narrower on the sides, with more fullness toward the back. Charles Frederick Worth made claim to the introduction of the hoop-supported skirt as well as the elongated skirt shape that replaced it.

William Morris is considered the father of the Arts and Crafts movement. Influenced by the earlier Romantic styles, he was among a group of artists who railed against the evils of modernity. Morris and his Pre-Raphaelite contemporaries were leading exponents of a school of design that called for a return to the guild system and valued the styles of the Middle Ages. This was an international movement in the decorative and fine arts that began in Britain and later flourished in Europe and North America. William Morris made furniture, decorative objects, wallpaper, fabrics, upholstery, and fireplace tiles.

This 1865 garment was worn by women with a leisurely lifestyle. The extremely tight corset narrowed their waists, which was made to seem even smaller with a large hooped petticoat. The extravagances in this fashion were not practical for the rapidly growing working classes.

The skirt of this cream ensemble with purple military trim has a slight pyramid style with a slightly flatter front and much fuller shape toward the back. This jacket and skirt were worn over a crinoline hooped petticoat. The silk fabric had a cream field with delicate lavender flowers and small green leaves. The silk cream colored fabric is 16 inches in width. The delicate flower patterns are reminiscent of tile patterns similar to many designed by William Morris.

The jacket has a distinct military influence with the horizontal use of braid and buttons. The peplum of the jacket is edged with purple fringe and two rows of purple velvet ribbon. Similar purple velvet trim is used along the cuff of the sleeves. The sleeves are finished with piped armscyes. A small watch pocket sits in the waist seam on the front left side of the jacket.

The full skirt hem is finished at the back with a 12-inch train. Note the center front skirt and center back pieces are rectangles with ten gores pulling the skirt to the back. Each skirt panel is flanked on one side with a selvage of the fabric and the other side with the diagonal-cut edge of the fabric. The panels are sewed selvage edge to diagonal edge. This process pulls the skirt toward the back, reinforcing the pyramid shape. When cutting the skirt panels, I noticed that two pieces can be spooned together and cut from one length of fabric as the spooned pieced together measure the 16-inch width. The skirt is closed with hooks and eyes on a petersham waistband. Purple velvet binding finishes the hem.

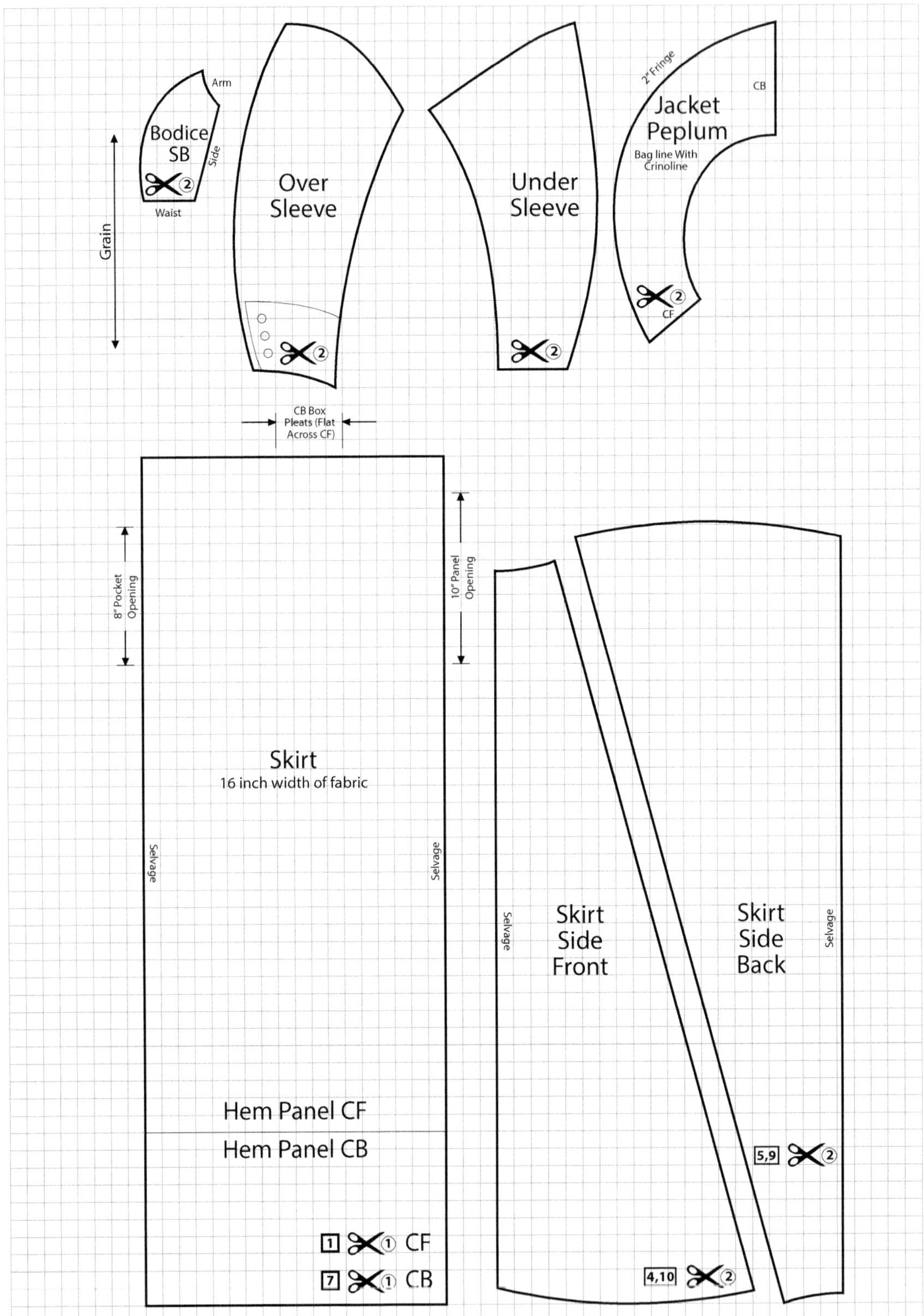

See photos for placement of trim

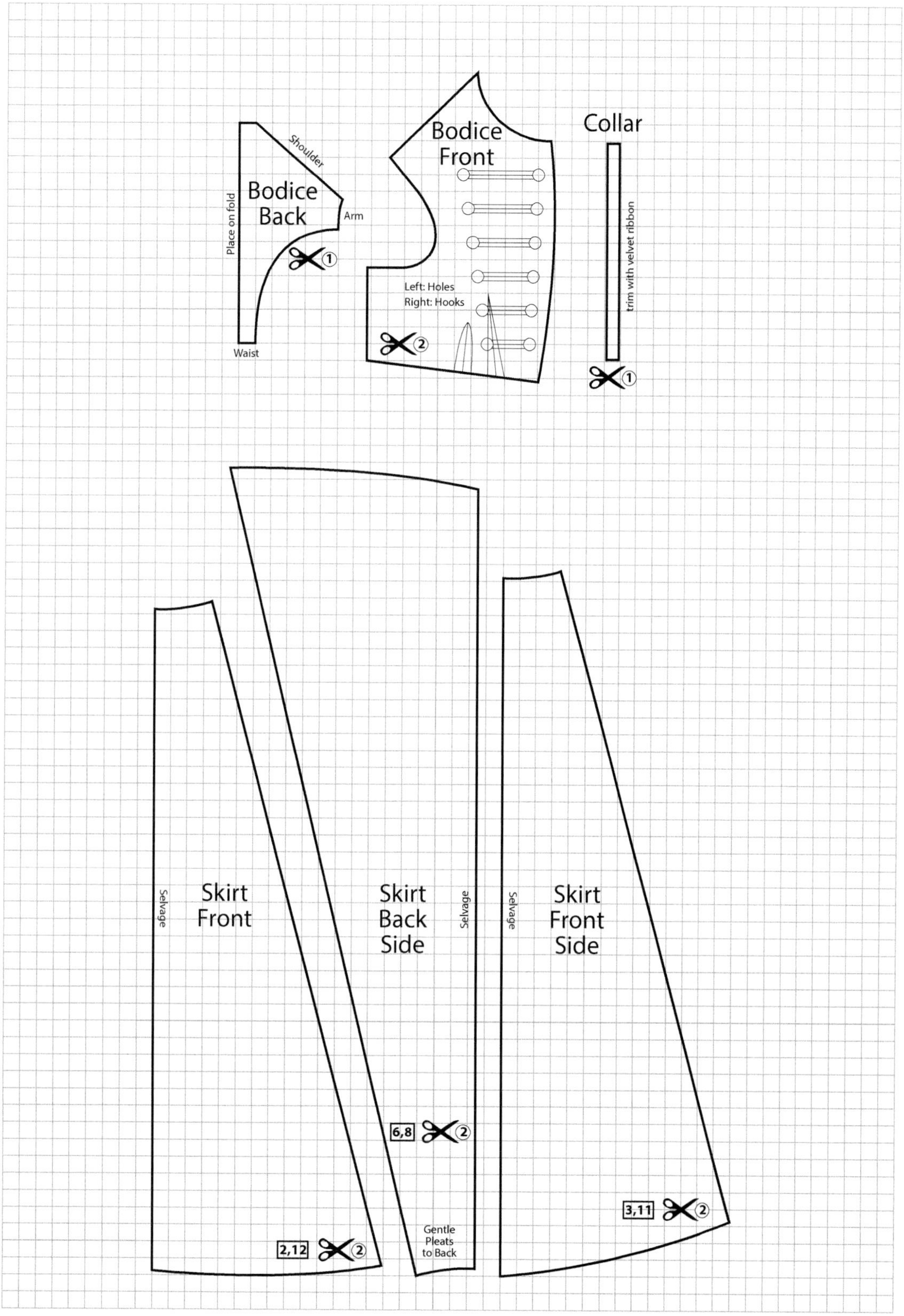

Bodice Back
Shoulder
Arm
Place on fold
Waist
1
Bodice Front
Left: Holes
Right: Hooks
2
Collar
trim with velvet ribbon
1
Skirt Front
Selvage
2,12
2
Skirt Back Side
Selvage
6,8
2
Gentle Pleats to Back
Skirt Front Side
Selvage
3,11
2

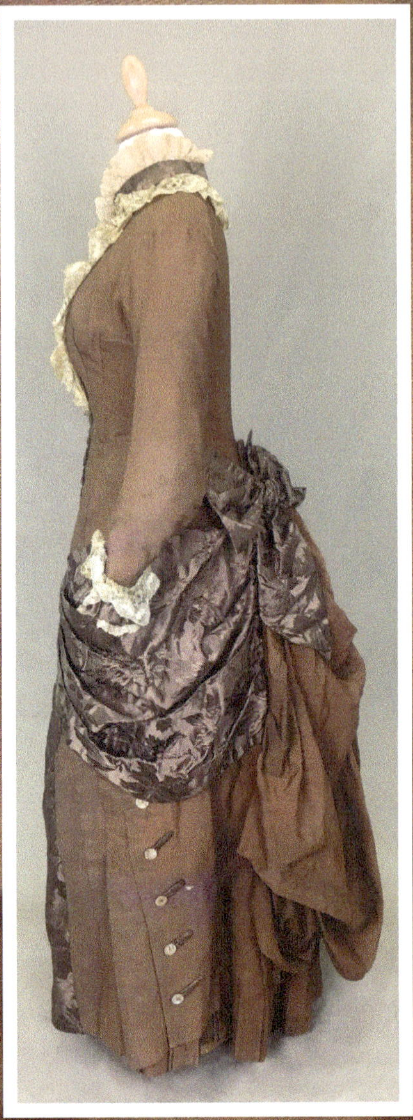

1875

Wool and Brocade Cuirass

By 1870, in Western countries, the shift from agrarian to urban industrial economies continued. Overcrowding, abject poverty, and unsanitary living conditions led to social unrest. Political action soon followed, to help the poor and alleviate unsafe working conditions. Many disillusioned people turned toward socialist ideals to fix society. Another new notion was put forward by Charles Darwin in *The Origin of the Species*. Many felt that Darwin was anti-Christian. Others looked at evolution as a model for progressive movement in society.

New inventions were a result of industrial progress. In 1876 the telephone was invented by Alexander Graham Bell. In 1877 Thomas Edison invented the phonograph and in 1879, the lightbulb. Box cameras became available to mass consumers and changed the way people chronicled their lives. In 1872 a steam-powered machine was developed for cutting multiple layers of cloth at one time. Mass production of clothing in sweatshops became common, with most of the sweatshop workers being women.

Widowed Queen Victoria was overshadowed by the social exploits of her eldest son, Edward. France entered the Belle Époque, an age of sophistication and elegance that kept Paris at the center of art and fashion until the First World War. After the Transcontinental Railroad was built, the urge to expand dominated

Asymmetrical hip bow

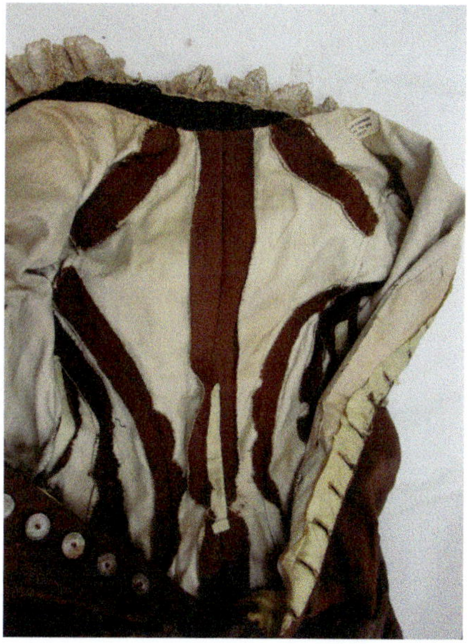

Inside bodice

U.S. thinking. Between 1876 and 1896, eight new states entered into the Union. The technological and organizational advances made during this period and the riches amassed gave this era its name: The Guilded Age.

In 1863 Ebenezer Butterick and his wife, Ellen Augusta Pollard Butterick, developed tissue paper dress patterns in various standard sizes. This revolutionized home sewing. As early as the 1840s, tissue paper patterns were available in Britain but the Buttericks successfully marketed them in the 1860s. The Butterick Company opened a branch on Regent Street in London in 1876.

Skirt bottom ruffle

Fashion magazines also produced paper patterns for beadwork, lace, knitting, and crochet. Many items from these patterns were used to make women's dress accessories.

It is an interesting contradiction that while a narrative of freedom was developing in society, clothing for a well-appointed woman was as restrictive as ever. In the 1870s and early 1880s women's skirts were held up in the back with a bustle cage or a bustle pad. This had evolved from the crinoline cage and was reconfigured to give the wearer a centaur-like silhouette. Between the previous two periods was a transition where a long, close-fitting, princess-line, cuirass-style bodice with no waist seam was worn, with a low small bustle at the back.

This bodice is well fitted to the figure with a center front closure of 15 mother-of-pearl ¾-inch buttons. The center front top of the bodice is finished with a V-shaped brown brocade bib and high stand collar. The collar has a ruffle of cream-colored lace on the base of the collar and at the top of the collar stand. The same lace forms a ruffle along the outside edge of the bib.

The curved, narrow two-pieced sleeves are brown wool and are set into the armscye with no fullness. They are finished at the cuff with three tiers of lace and brocade. The first tier is the same lace as the collar and bib and sits up on the sleeve. The second tier is brocade smocked at its base. It sits facing down the sleeve. The third tier, closest to the wrist, is also a cream lace ruffle. There is a small watch pocket hidden on the left side of the horizontal waist seam on the left side of the bodice.

The front of the skirt has an A-line shaped pane[1] of brown brocade. The sides of the skirt are four large vertical knife pleats of the brown wool facing the front. The side-to-side back is a panel of brown wool with an asymmetrical hem, lower in the front than the back. This panel has four decorative buttons and false sutache button holes. These four buttons and trim sit one atop another at the side of the skirt panel. The back bottom of the skirt finishes with a row of wool 7-inch-wide double box pleats. Across the skirt front, from hip to upper leg, is a swag of brown brocade. It is caught up in the center front with a large rosette of brown brocade. The draped bustle in the back of the skirt is a large bag of wool that sits asymmetrically across the back. Also across the left back top is a 12-inch-wide brocade bow that is attached at an angle. The bow has one bag lined tail.

Skirt bottom center front

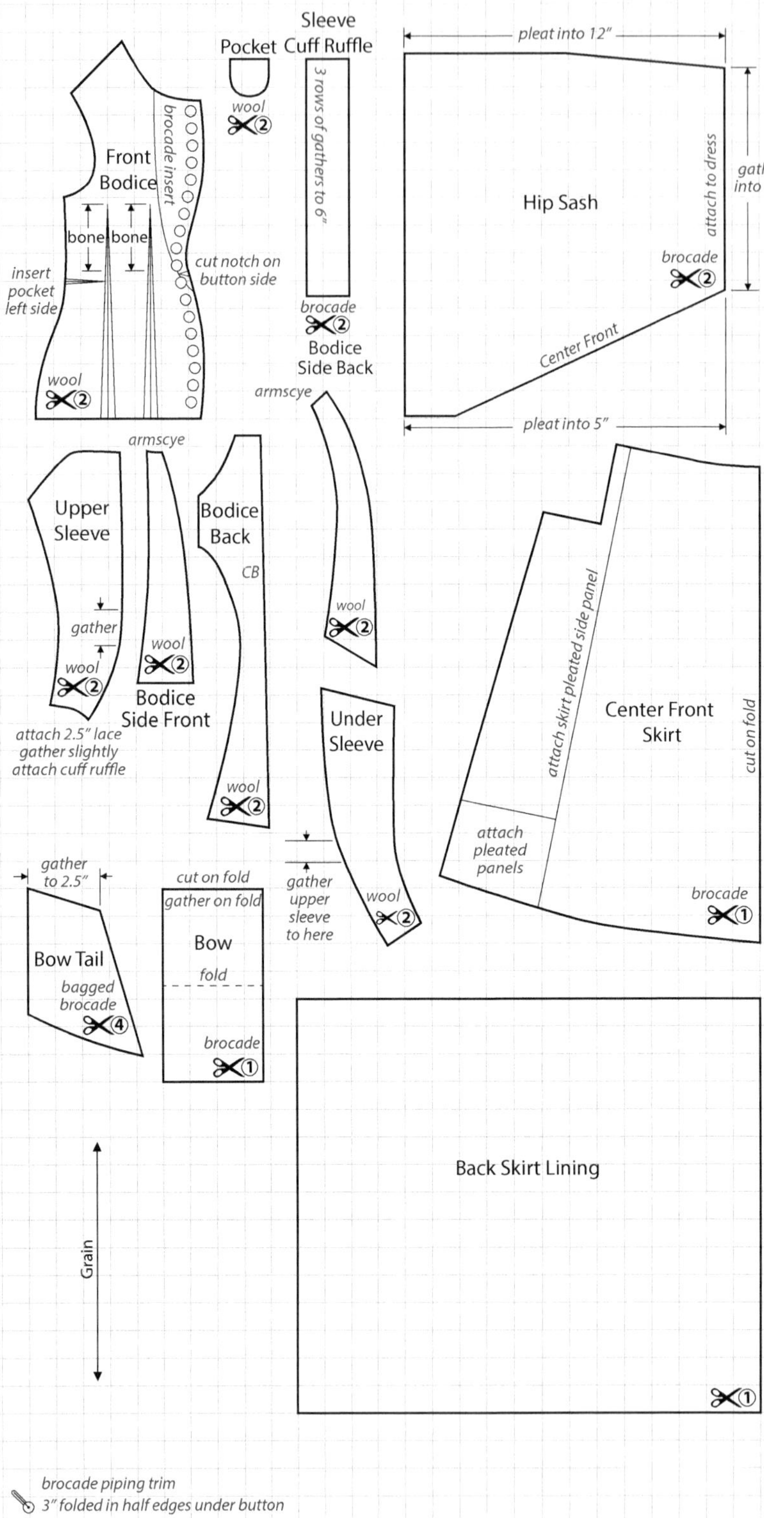
Front Bodice
brocade insert
bone
bone
insert pocket left side
cut notch on button side
wool
Pocket
wool
Sleeve Cuff Ruffle
3 rows of gathers to 6″
brocade
Bodice Side Back
armscye
pleat into 12″
Hip Sash
attach to dress
gather into 17″
brocade
Center Front
pleat into 5″
armscye
Upper Sleeve
gather
wool
attach 2.5″ lace
gather slightly
attach cuff ruffle
wool
Bodice Side Front
Bodice Back
CB
wool
wool
Under Sleeve
gather upper sleeve to here
wool
attach skirt pleated side panel
Center Front Skirt
cut on fold
attach pleated panels
brocade
gather to 2.5″
Bow Tail
bagged brocade
cut on fold
gather on fold
Bow
fold
brocade
Back Skirt Lining
Grain
brocade piping trim
3″ folded in half edges under button

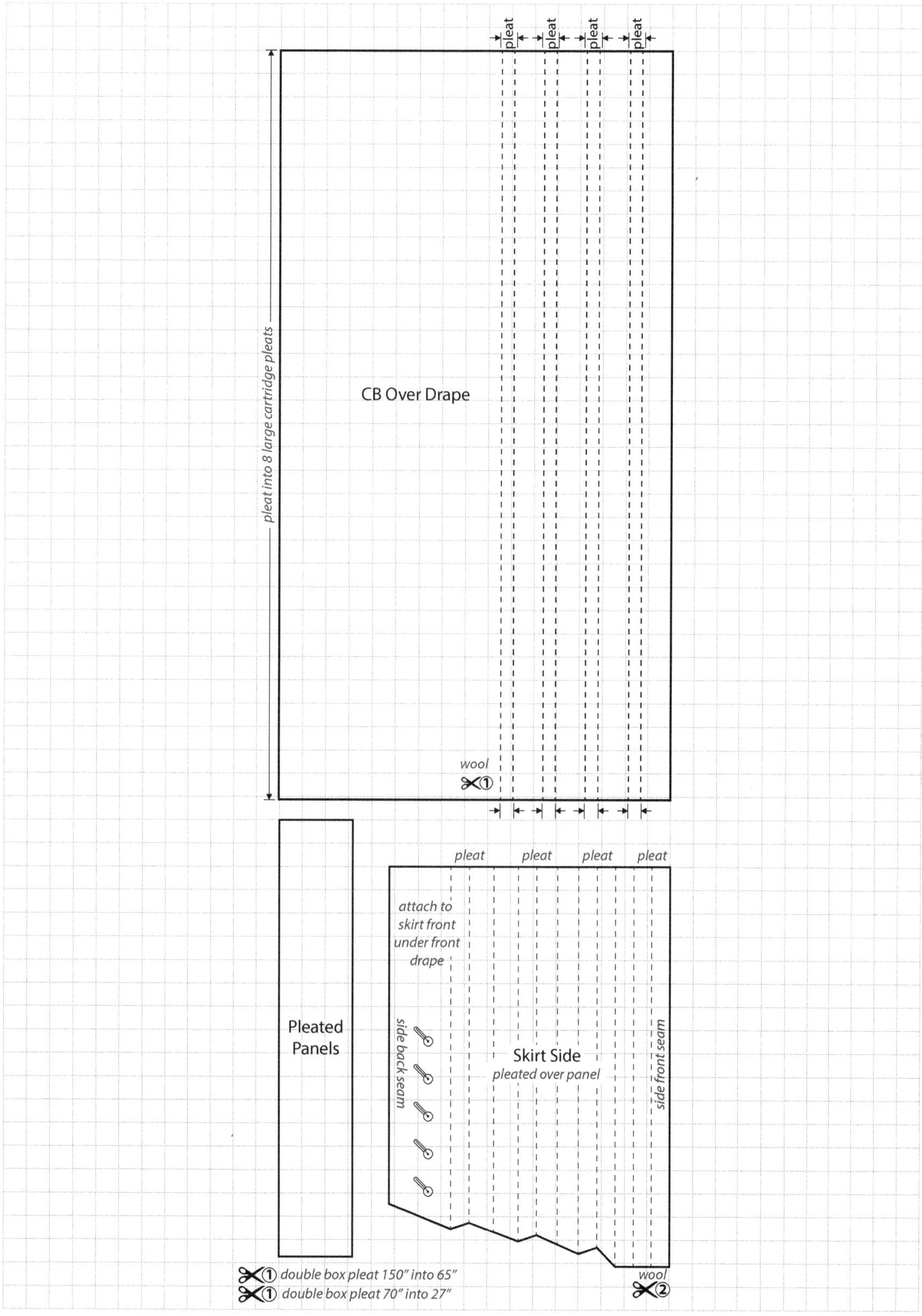
pleat
pleat
pleat
pleat
pleat into 8 large cartridge pleats
CB Over Drape
wool
✂①
Pleated Panels
pleat
pleat
pleat
pleat
attach to skirt front under front drape
side back seam
Skirt Side
pleated over panel
side front seam
wool
✂②
✂① double box pleat 150″ into 65″
✂① double box pleat 70″ into 27″

1889

Silk Ensemble with Black Faceted Beads

This 1889 red silk ensemble is an interesting transition between styles. It is at the tail end of the bustle era and the nascent silhouette of the 1890s. The bodice and skirt have a slight bustle ruffle at the base of the back. The full sleeves are a two-piece unit that are gathered at the cap of the sleeve and at both the outside and inside of the elbow bend. In the 1890s this will become much fuller in the cap of the sleeve.

The bodice is pleated and bloused from neck to waist, hiding a hook and eye closure panel. The hooks and eyes are switched back and forth on each side (see image that includes the hook and eyes). This arrangement would have prevented the hook and eyes from becoming undone inside of the folds.

The neck is finished with a curved stand collar edged with a thin, black, box-pleated lace that sits up high at the back of the neck. The collar is scattered with square, faceted black beads.

The bodice front and back, at the wrist of the sleeves, the collar, and the attached belt are scattered with the black, square, facetted beads. The bodice is attached to back tails that appear to be part of the back of the skirt. The tails splay over an under-panel of black flocked velvet floral ending in the short train. The

Side shoulder and collar

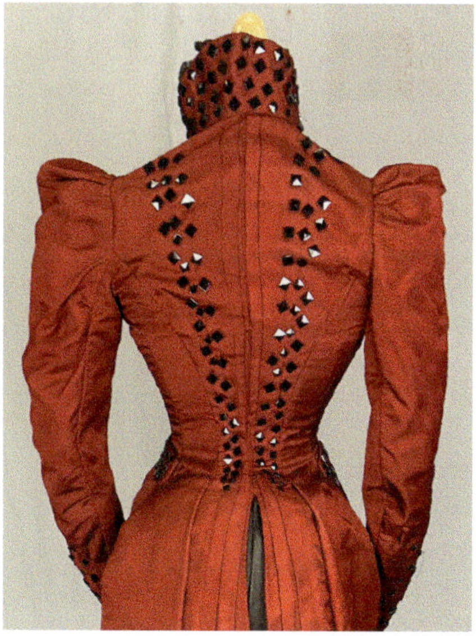

Back bodice

Hook and eye arrangement

front of the skirt is quite straight, flaring a bit at the sides.

This ensemble has an hourglass shape emphasized with a chevron-shaped belt. The V-shaped belt is sewn at the side back of the jacket and curves down to create a pointed front. The belt is made from the red silk and also covered with the black beads. The center back of the bodice is completed with securely sewed back pleats.

The bottom of the skirt is finished with a 2½-inch black knife-pleated ruffle all around the front of the red skirt and around the black back underskirt.

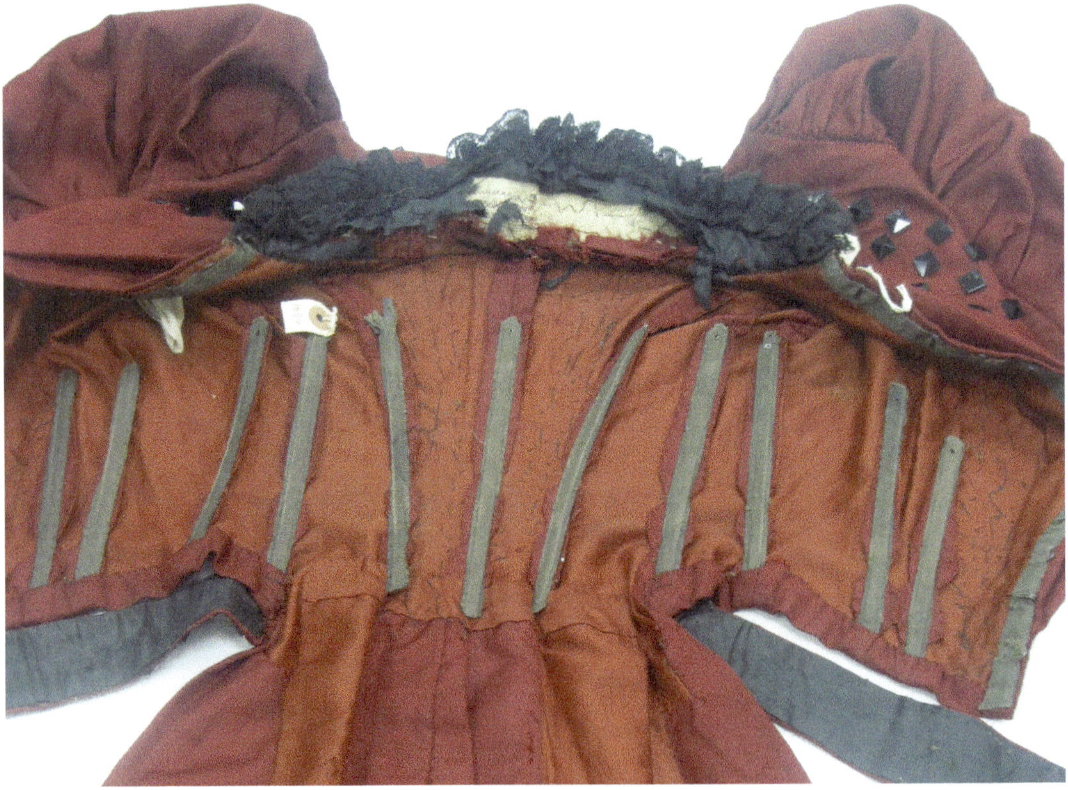

Bodice lining

Bodice tails *Side*

Skirt bottom knife-pleated ruffle

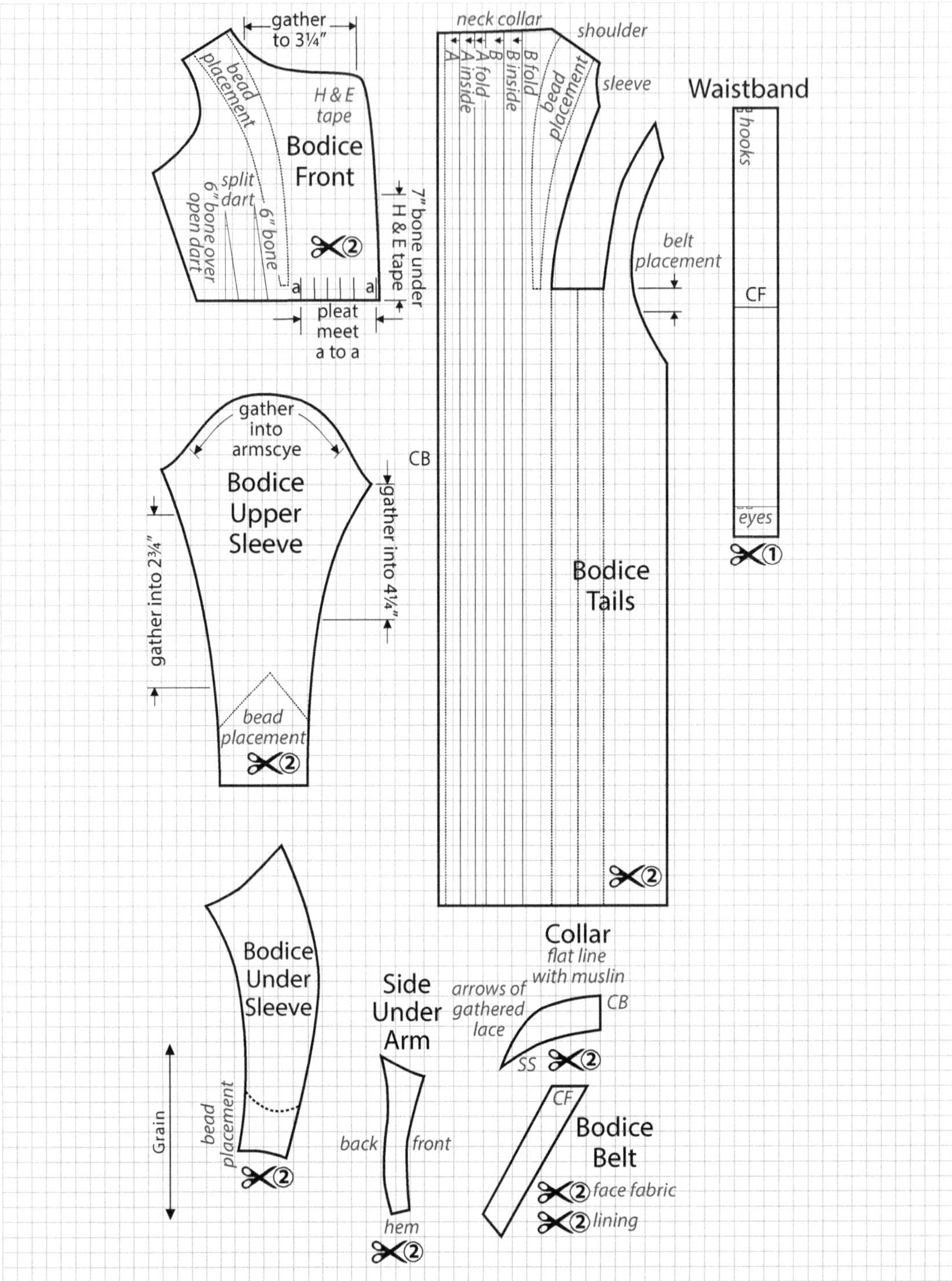
gather to 3¼″
bead placement
H & E tape
Bodice Front
split dart
6″ bone over open dart
6″ bone
a
a
7″ bone under H & E tape
pleat meet a to a
neck collar
shoulder
A
A inside
A fold
B
B inside
B fold
bead placement
sleeve
Waistband
hooks
belt placement
CF
gather into armscye
Bodice Upper Sleeve
CB
gather into 2¾″
gather into 4¼″
eyes
Bodice Tails
bead placement
Bodice Under Sleeve
Grain
bead placement
Side Under Arm
back
front
hem
Collar
flat line with muslin
arrows of gathered lace
CB
SS
CF
Bodice Belt
face fabric
lining

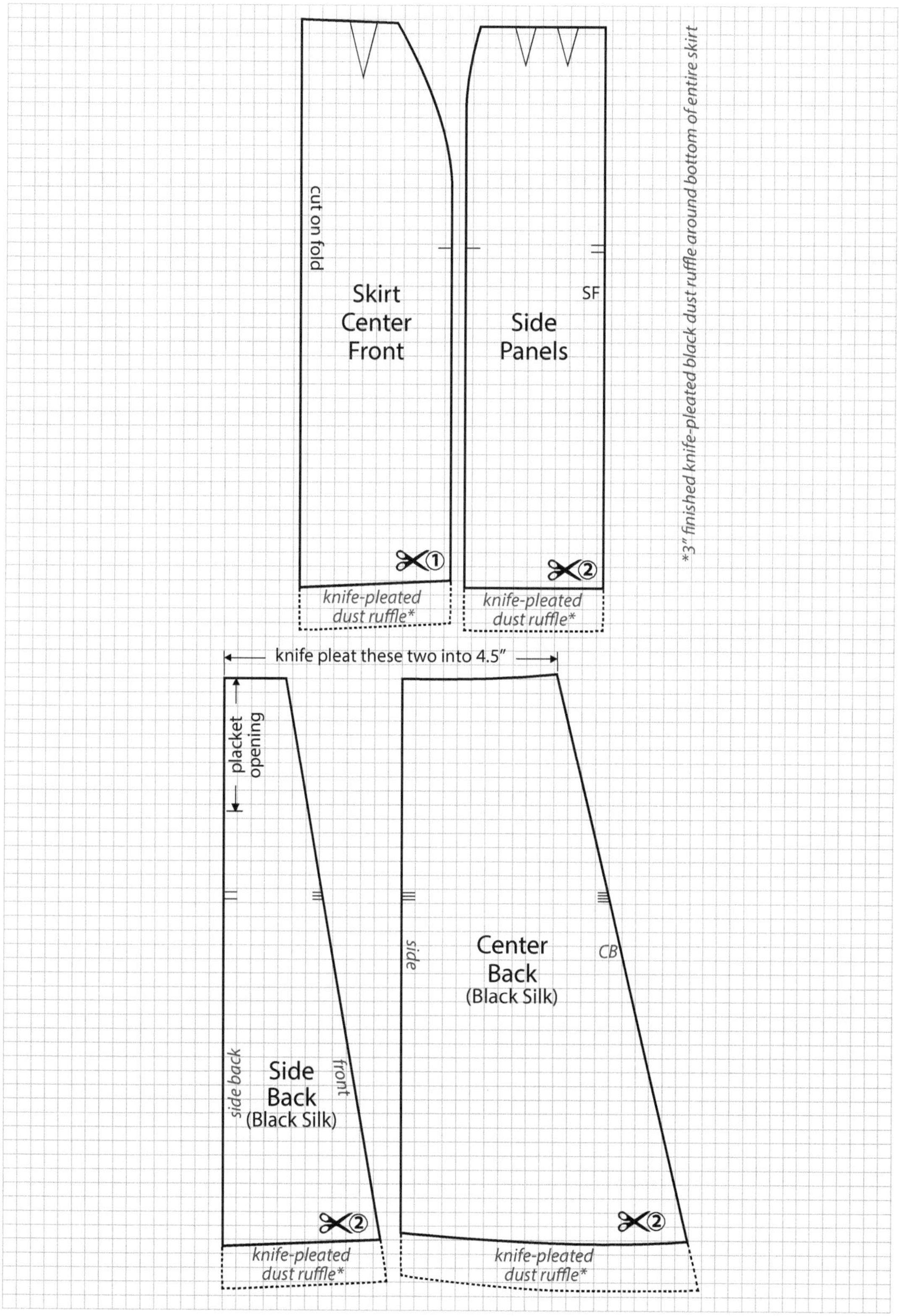
cut on fold
Skirt Center Front
knife-pleated dust ruffle*
SF
Side Panels
knife-pleated dust ruffle*
*3" finished knife-pleated black dust ruffle around bottom of entire skirt
knife pleat these two into 4.5"
placket opening
side back
Side Back (Black Silk)
front
knife-pleated dust ruffle*
side
Center Back (Black Silk)
CB
knife-pleated dust ruffle*

1898

Wool Tartan and Military Trim

In the 1880s and 1890s the telephone began to work its way into every business. The typewriting machine was operated by typewriters (eventually known as typists), often women. The bicycle introduced great freedom of mobility, especially for women as cycling's popularity expanded.

A new breed of woman was making her mark on society. In the 1890s, the artist Alphonse Mucha was famous for his commercial posters. His signature style enveloped sinewy curves of Art Nouveau, marrying rigid tradition with playful movement, not unlike the newly gained flexibility and freedom women found with the bicycle.

By the 1870s, women had new career opportunities. The need for public school teachers provided justification for college education for women. During the Crimean and American Civil Wars, women's traditional roles of nursing family members at home was extended to battlefields.

A tradition of female activism in charitable organizations laid the foundation for women as professional social workers. "The New Woman" broke with convention by working outside the home and/or becoming politically active in the women's suffrage movement.

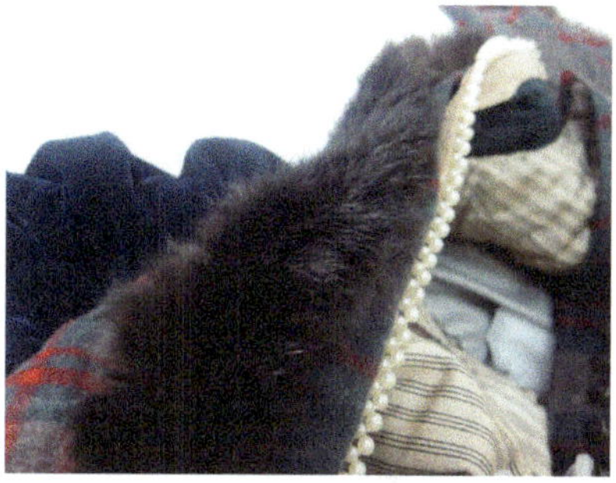

Fur and beaded stand collar

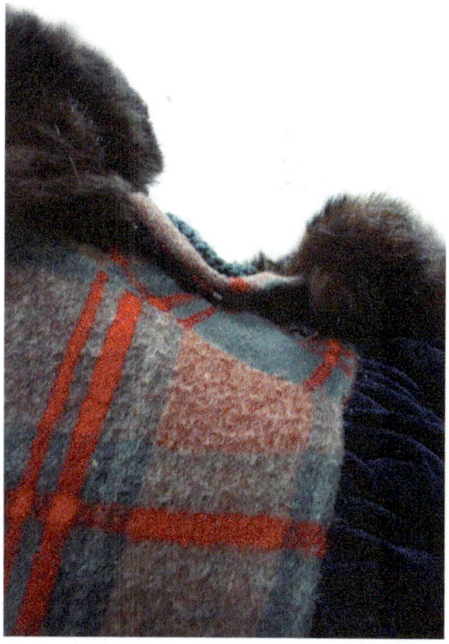

Shoulder closure

The large leg-o-mutton sleeves, small waist, and cone-shaped skirt inspired the phrase the "hourglass figure." The restrictive, tightly corseted torso, full skirt and outsized sleeves are an interesting counterpoint to some of the advances in the lives of women, albeit less restrictive than the bustle style. The broad sleeves did, however, give an authoritative, broad-shouldered silhouette. The cone-shape skirt gave women free leg movement.

In 1898 this tartan suit was made at the time of British/South African conflicts. The asymmetrical jacket panel and the swags of teal cording are similar to the cording on a man's military dress uniform.

This suit features a green/tan/red wool tartan jacket and separate skirt. The jacket has teal velvet leg-o-mutton sleeves. The jacket is closed at the front with twenty-one ½-inch shank buttons. It has a diagonal over-panel running from the right shoulder to the left hip. The closure and stand collar are trimmed with fur and the edge of the collar has a line of pearl-beaded trim. The jacket is lined with cotton twill. An inner waistband closes with a hook and eye. This inner waistband is attached to the inside of the jacket at the center inside back.

Teal color also appears with the velvet sleeves. They are quite full, with 54 inches across the sleeve cap. The sleeves are flatlined with muslin and trimmed with dark fur around the wrists.

The center front of the skirt is a rectangle. The two gored back skirt pieces have fan pleats across the back. The bottom of the skirt is also finished in dark fur. Below the finished edge of the hem is a dark green horse hair braid sewed on half an inch lower than the hem to protect the hem from wear.

Bodice center back

Horse hair at bottom of hem

Asymmetrical front closure

Inside jacket boned seams

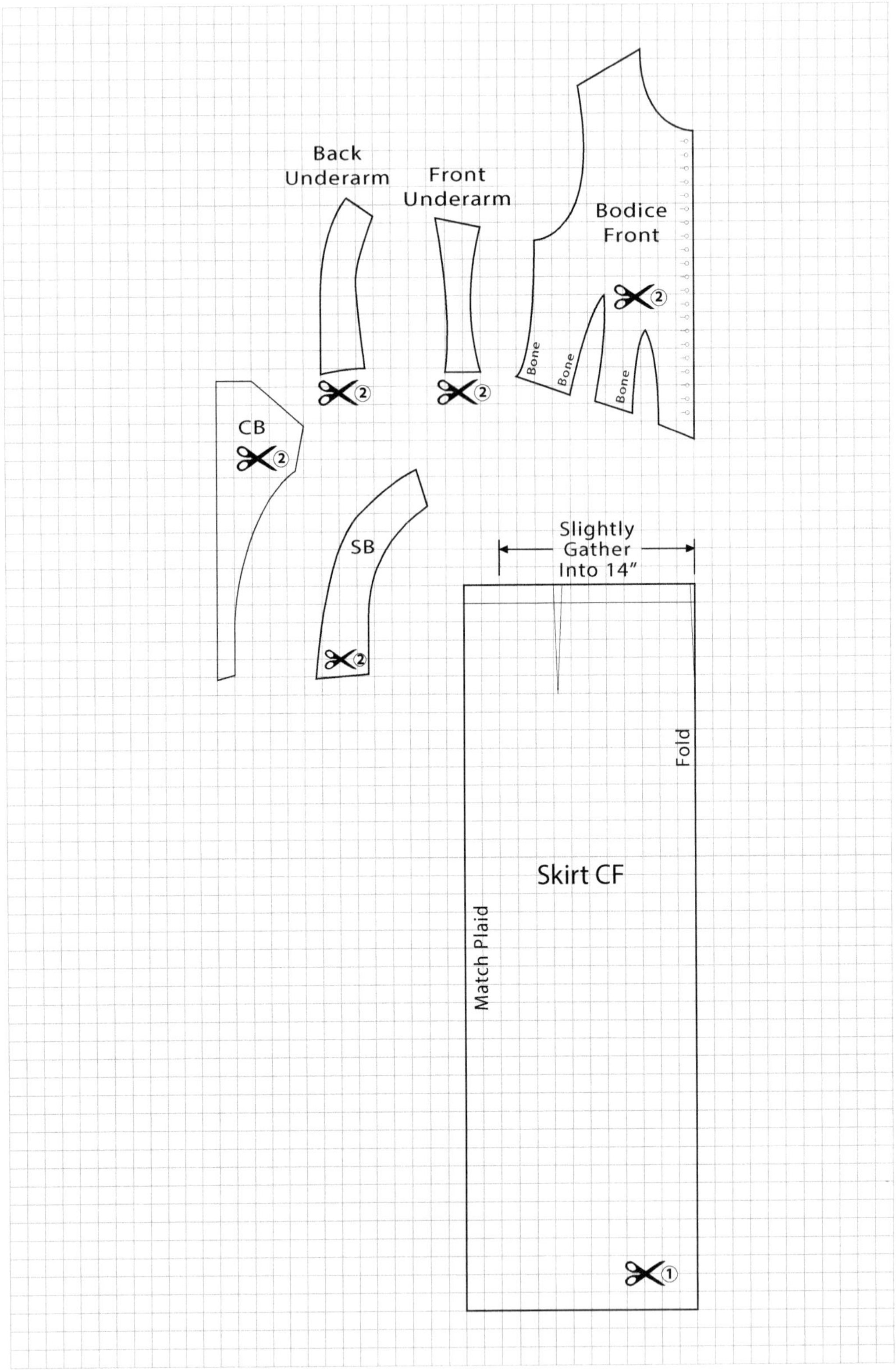
Back Underarm
Front Underarm
Bodice Front
Bone
Bone
Bone
CB
SB
Slightly Gather Into 14"
Fold
Skirt CF
Match Plaid

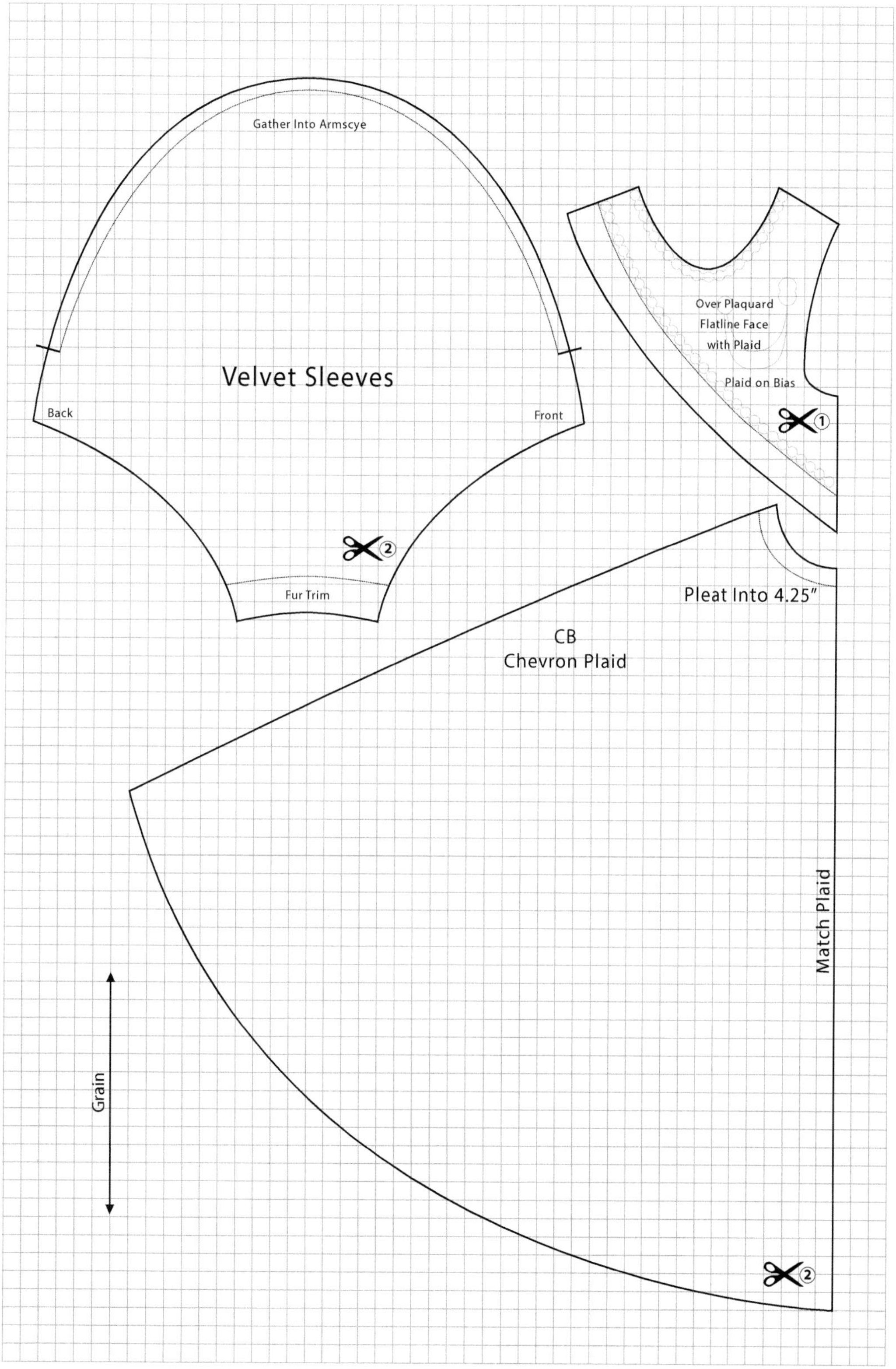
Gather Into Armscye
Velvet Sleeves
Back
Front
Fur Trim
Over Plaquard
Flatline Face
with Plaid
Plaid on Bias
Pleat Into 4.25″
CB
Chevron Plaid
Match Plaid
Grain

1902

Wool Tennis Dress

Queen Victoria died in 1901. Edward the VII came to the throne at age 59 and reigned until 1910. In the brief Edwardian reign, the king and his socially elite friends followed the art and fashions of other European countries. Edward enjoyed travelling and his visits to Paris improved relations between France and Britain. Paris remained the center of fashion and the elegant salons of the French couture houses were a Mecca for fashionable women all over the world.

The sinuous lines of the Art Nouveau style were emulated in the shape of early 20th century women's clothing. A rigid s-bend corset forced a pigeon-breasted silhouette. A popular hair style continued the Art Nouveau lines with billowing upswept waves. The American illustrator Charles Dana Gibson drew a mono-bosomed beauty, soon known as "the Gibson Girl." Cecil Beaton described this silhouette as ladies "laced into corsets that gave them pouter-pigeon bosoms and protruding posteriors."

In the late 19th century, women began to regularly gain access to higher education. With that came exposure to a variety of sports. As more women became involved in physical activity, they became more competitive. Croquet, bowling, archery, and tennis were the sports of choice.

Collar

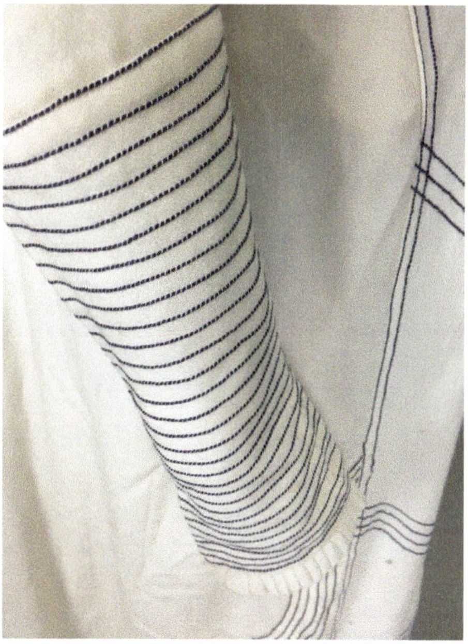

Lower sleeves

Cuff net and lower sleeve

Center front and side skirt

In the summer of 1900, sailing made its appearance as an Olympic sport. Women and children's clothing often sported nautical motifs in blues and whites. The blue and white color scheme on this tennis frock can also suggest playful seaside summer activity.

This lightweight cream wool blouse and separate skirt was intended to be worn for tennis. Wearing an s-bend corset and a skirt with a train suggest a genteel version of the game.

The bodice of this Edwardian ensemble is puffed into the pigeon-breasted shape. The nautical theme is seen with the stylized waves emphasized in navy blue decorative stitching. The neckline is finished with a tapered collar . The skirt fits over the hips and ends in a short train.

The bodice and skirt are trimmed with navy blue couching. The couching emphasizes the pin tucks down the front of the bodice, the fullness of the sleeves, and the cylindrical lines around the lower arm. It also emphasizes the large chevrons down the front, the side front, and bottom of the skirt. The tapered collar repeats the wave motif and comes to a point on either side of the neck. The bodice yoke front has a square shape that is reminiscent of a sailor-style collar. The shape is emphasized with repeated rows of the couching.

The upper sleeve of the two-piece sleeves are pin-tucked into the armscye. The pin tucks are double top-stitched with couching and finished half way down the upper arm with a small white decorative button. The couching is connected under the button. The edges of the sleeves are finished with a double row of one inch tiny knife pleated cream colored net.

The top of the skirt sits both straight and smooth down the front and sides, with a slight fullness at the back waistband. A stylized wave motif flanks the vertical sides and around the back of the skirt. Each tip of the wave-like shapes is emphasized with a couched button. The skirt sits at the floor in the front and slightly trains in the back. There is a 10-inch ruffle that runs under the front panel and around the underside of the back of the skirt to help support the train.

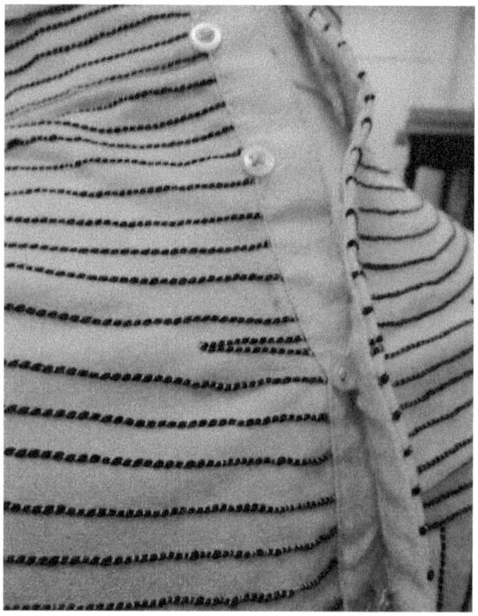

Back neck

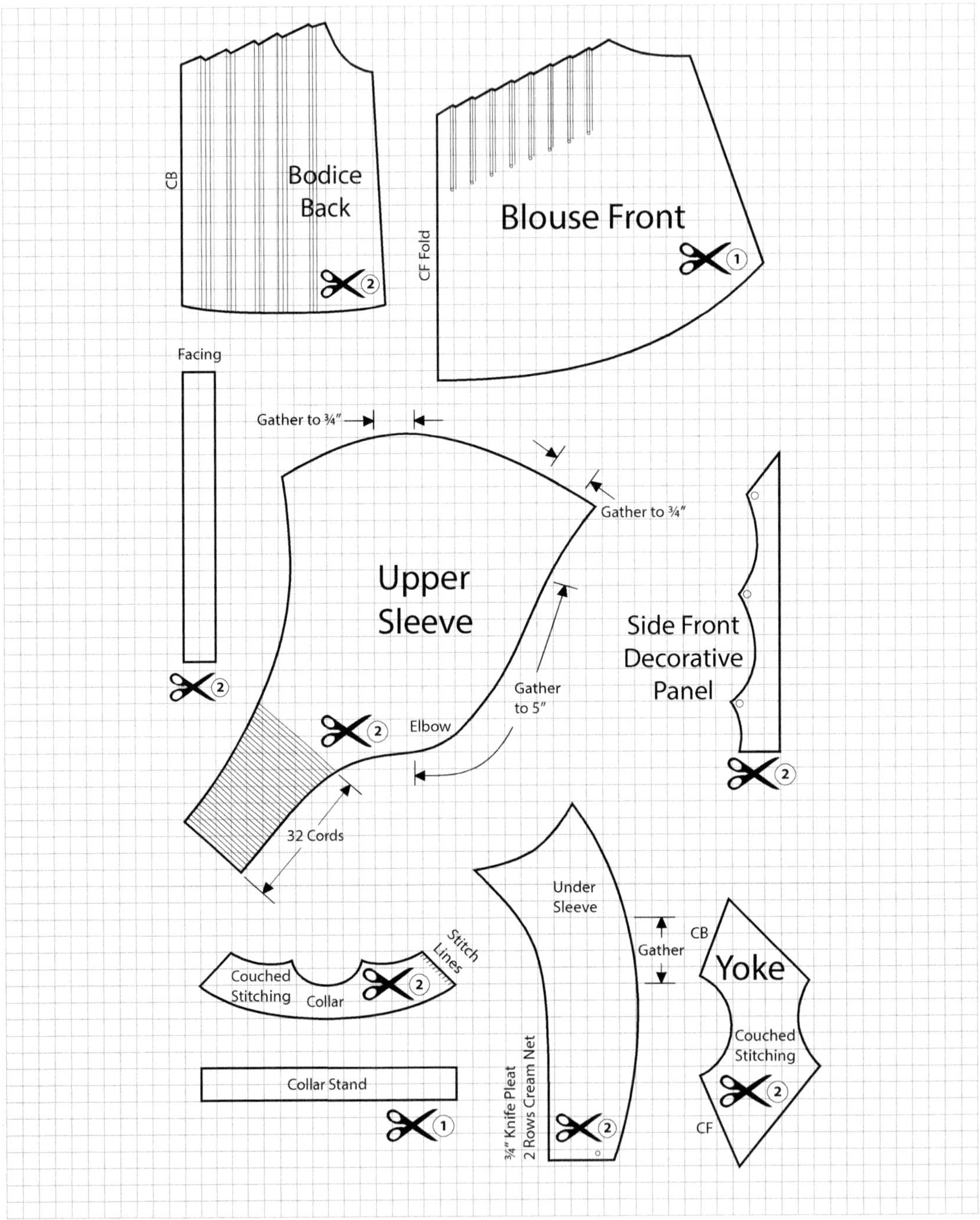

Bodice
Back
CB
Blouse Front
CF Fold
Facing
Gather to ¾″
Gather to ¾″
Upper
Sleeve
Side Front
Decorative
Panel
Gather
to 5″
Elbow
32 Cords
Under
Sleeve
CB
Gather
Yoke
Stitch
Lines
Couched
Stitching
Collar
Couched
Stitching
Collar Stand
¾″ Knife Pleat
2 Rows Cream Net
CF

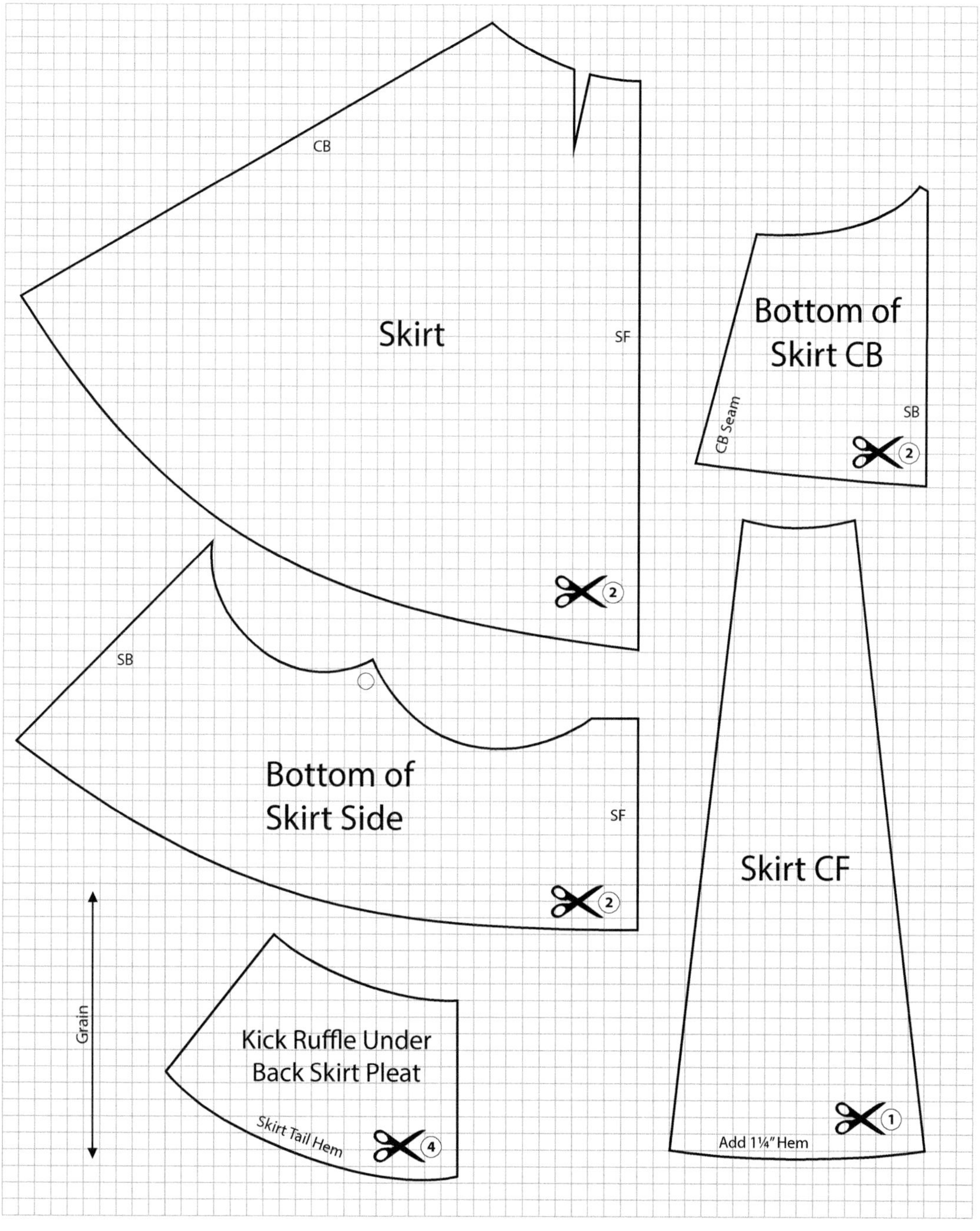
Skirt
CB
SF
2
Bottom of Skirt CB
CB Seam
SB
2
Bottom of Skirt Side
SB
SF
2
Skirt CF
Add 1¼" Hem
1
Kick Ruffle Under Back Skirt Pleat
Skirt Tail Hem
4
Grain

1908

Silk and Lace Evening Dress

During the first decade of the 20th century, world-wide trade became extensive. Railways were built in both developed and underdeveloped countries. Germany had become a military and ecomonic power. The United States had become an industrial giant.

By 1908, on both sides of the Atlantic, railway travel was routine and Henry Ford's Model "T" became the first mass-produced automobile. Telephones, electricity, and gas lines were being installed in middle-class homes. In 1908 a patent was taken out on the first portable vacuum cleaner. Couples danced to the music of a wind-up gramophone in their living rooms and attended dark theaters to watch the flickering images of moving pictures. Invisible words traveled across the oceans with Marconi's wireless telegraph.

Most middle- and upper-class women could still expect to lead their lives as housewives and mothers. Life for them was mainly tied to domesticity. Their place was still in the home. Big changes were on the horizon.

In the summer of 1908, London hosted the Olympics. For the first time 37 women participated in the Olympic

Bodice lace appliques

Sleeve net and lace appliques

Games. Increased literacy among middle-class women gave them wider access to information and ideas. New magazines marketed to women appealed to their tastes and helped define modern femininity.

The invention of the typewriter and telephone increased employment opportunities for women. The rapid expansion of the school system increased the number of women in various occupations. As middle-class women rose in status they insisted on a political voice. By 1908 the women's suffrage movement picked up steam.

This steel blue silk gown is trimmed with cream lace. It has a high neck, slim sleeves, and a skirt that fits over the hips and flares slightly at the hem. The inner waistband label is "T & L Bacon, Liverpool."

In this time of great change, this 1908 dress shows both old-fashioned taste and new progressive style lines. The silhouette of the dress is much narrower than earlier in the decade. The straighter lines of the skirt contrast with the heavy, Victorian-style lace which encircles the neck and flanks the shoulders. This dress combines light netting with heavy lace appliques. The shoulders and arms are covered with the netting that revealed the collar bone, shoulder, and arm skin. The skirt combines thick silk panels (front and back) lined from bust to hem with several dozen covered buttons. Buttons under other circumstances would tightly close a dress but these are merely decoration. This dress appears to straddle the tight, restricted Victorian ideal with looser, softer qualities. It is a perfect transition piece between the repressive 19th century and the progressive 20th century.

The bodice is blue silk with a center front silk panel from bust to hem. From waist to waist and over the shoulders are panels of silk and lace that spill over the

Designer label

Yoke lace

top of the sleeves. The bodice is made of net covered with lace above the bust and up the stand collar. There is a petersham inner waistband. The center front silk panel and the lace bodice are closed at the back with a series of hooks and eyes. The ¾-length sleeves are a combination of net and lace that end at the wrist in a double net ruffle. The skirt slightly flares with a silk center panel running down the bodice and continues to the hem at the front and back. Both front and back silk panels are flanked with pairs of decorative blue silk covered buttons. Large lace appliques cover the top front panel, sit out over the shoulder panels, and run along both the side and back of the skirt.

Center back button panel released to show center back hook and eye

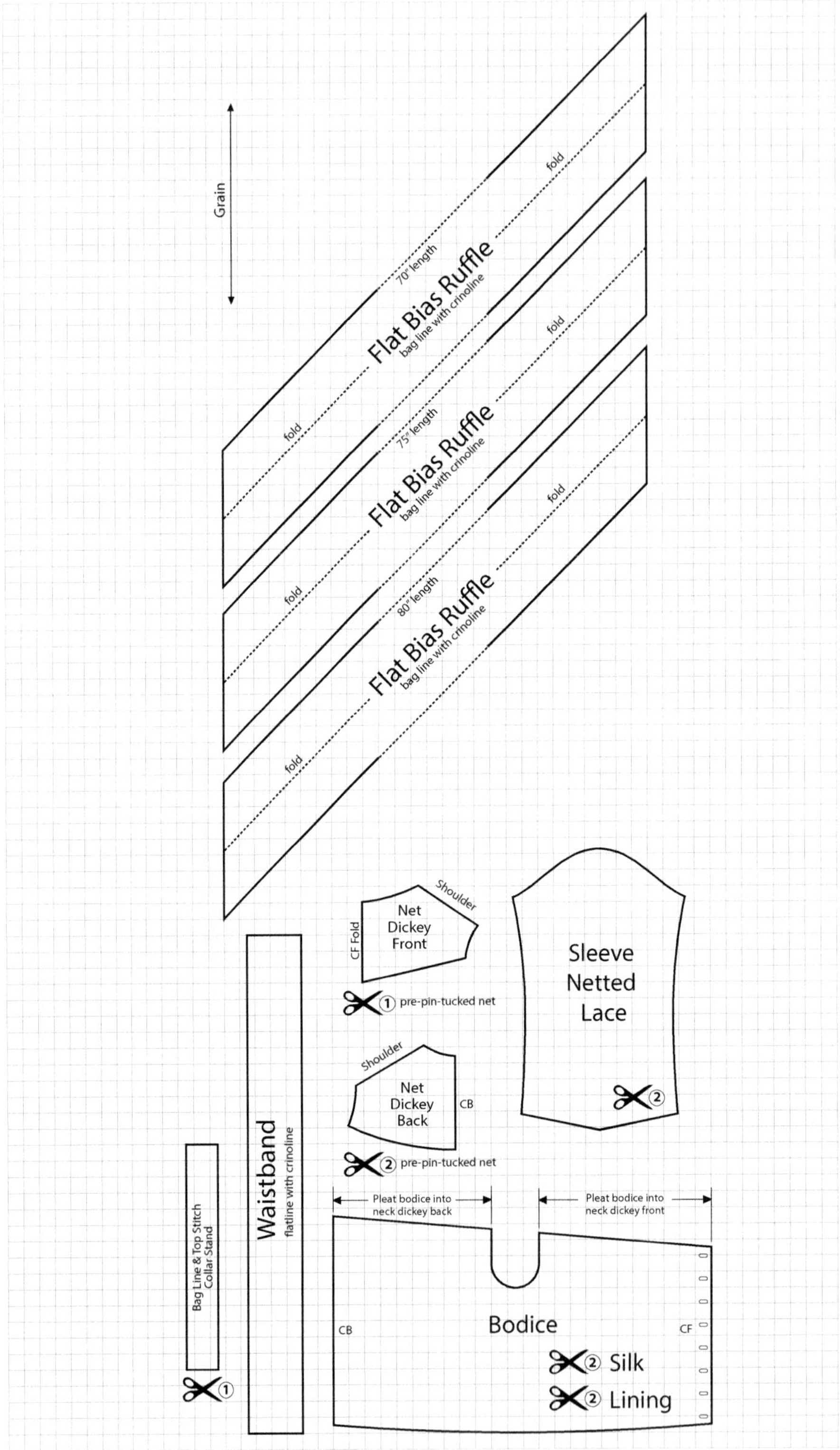
Grain
Flat Bias Ruffle
bag line with crinoline
70" length
fold
fold
Flat Bias Ruffle
bag line with crinoline
75" length
fold
fold
Flat Bias Ruffle
bag line with crinoline
80" length
fold
fold
Net
Dickey
Front
CF Fold
Shoulder
1 pre-pin-tucked net
Sleeve
Netted
Lace
2
Net
Dickey
Back
Shoulder
CB
2 pre-pin-tucked net
Bag Line & Top Stitch
Collar Stand
1
Waistband
flatline with crinoline
Pleat bodice into
neck dickey back
Pleat bodice into
neck dickey front
Bodice
CB
CF
2 Silk
2 Lining

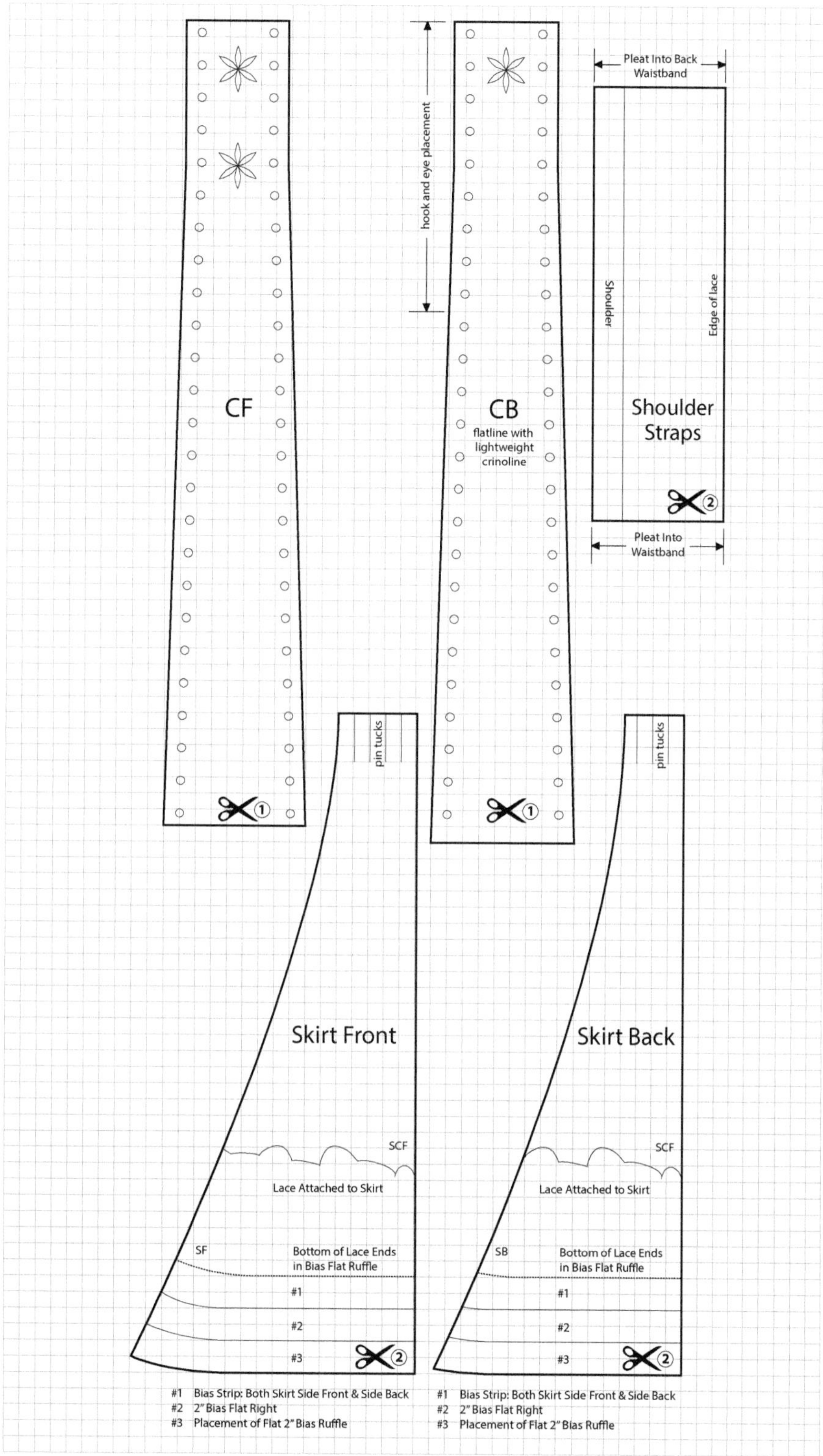
hook and eye placement
CF
CB
flatline with
lightweight
crinoline
Pleat Into Back
Waistband
Shoulder
Edge of lace
Shoulder
Straps
Pleat Into
Waistband
pin tucks
pin tucks
Skirt Front
Skirt Back
SCF
SCF
Lace Attached to Skirt
Lace Attached to Skirt
SF
SB
Bottom of Lace Ends
in Bias Flat Ruffle
Bottom of Lace Ends
in Bias Flat Ruffle
#1
#2
#3
#1 Bias Strip: Both Skirt Side Front & Side Back
#2 2" Bias Flat Right
#3 Placement of Flat 2" Bias Ruffle
#1 Bias Strip: Both Skirt Side Front & Side Back
#2 2" Bias Flat Right
#3 Placement of Flat 2" Bias Ruffle

1910

Cotton Dress with Lace Inserts

By 1910, America had experienced big social changes caused by a huge influx of immigrants. Britain welcomed a new monarch, King George V. France was a center of creative thinking in music and the arts.

In 1911, the New York City Triangle Shirtwaist Factory fire killed 146, mostly young women. In the aftermath of this tragedy, improved working conditions and factory safety received press attention and government regulation.

General Motors introduced the electric self-starter for automobiles and Willis Carrier invented the air conditioner. Irving Berlin had his first big hit with *Alexander's Ragtime Band.* In 1909, Marie Curie became the first woman to receive the Nobel Prize in Chemistry and defined an international standard for radioactive emissions. European leaders were sparking with friction as Germany and France engaged in an armaments race that led to the Great War.

In 1910, the French fashion designer Paul Poiret, and much of the Parisian Fashion world, was inspired by the costume designs of Leon Bakst for the Ballet Russe in a production of *Scheherazade.* Those costumes

Bodice

Top of skirt panel

Bodice top

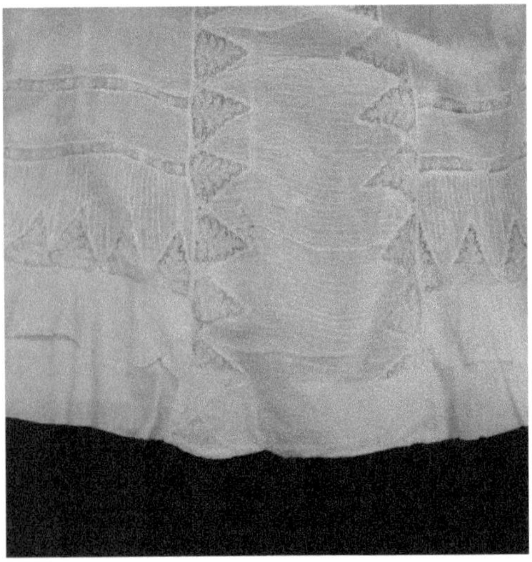

Skirt bottom

emphasized soft tunic-shaped garments from *The Arabian Nights*. Soon fashion included all things Middle or Far Eastern. The Middle East captured the imaginations of the fashion world, and in turn, influenced women's dress outside of France. At this time, Paul Poiret also advocated the elimination of the corset. What Poiret started in 1910 would be completed by the necessities brought on by the First World War.

This cotton and lace dress from 1910 marks the beginnings of twentieth-century fashion. The delicate, loose bodice of this cotton and lace dress with its ¾-length sleeves has just a hint of Asian fashion about it. The slightly A-lined silhouette remained in style until 1914.

This dress has a looser silhouette than earlier fashions. The decorative elements are a combination of the intricate use of lace triangles, pin tucks and lace ribbons. These details take the complexities of the past and use them in the relaxed manner of the modern era.

The bodice front has 18 small vertical pin tucks. Lace triangles and lace ribbons circle the neck. Five vertical lace ribbons run down the bodice front. The bodice back has similar pin tucks, lace ribbons, and lace triangle inserts.

The sleeves are also a combination of cotton, lace ribbon, and inserts of lace triangles. The ¾-length sleeves end in a cuff of cotton fabric, lace ribbon, lace triangles, and an edge ruffle of gathered lace ribbon.

The skirt waistband has a center horizontal insert of lace ribbon flanked top and bottom with the lightweight cotton pin tucks. The skirt has seven gored panels. The center front gore consists of waist-to-hem horizontal pin tucks with the edge of the gore outlined with lace triangles that point toward the center front of the skirt. The other six gores have two lines of ribbon lace inserted along the bottom. The six back gores are finished with two 3-inch flat bias tucks.

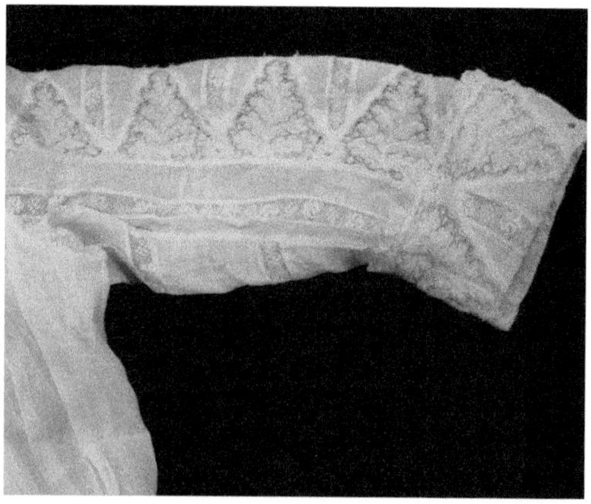

Sleeve

Waistband

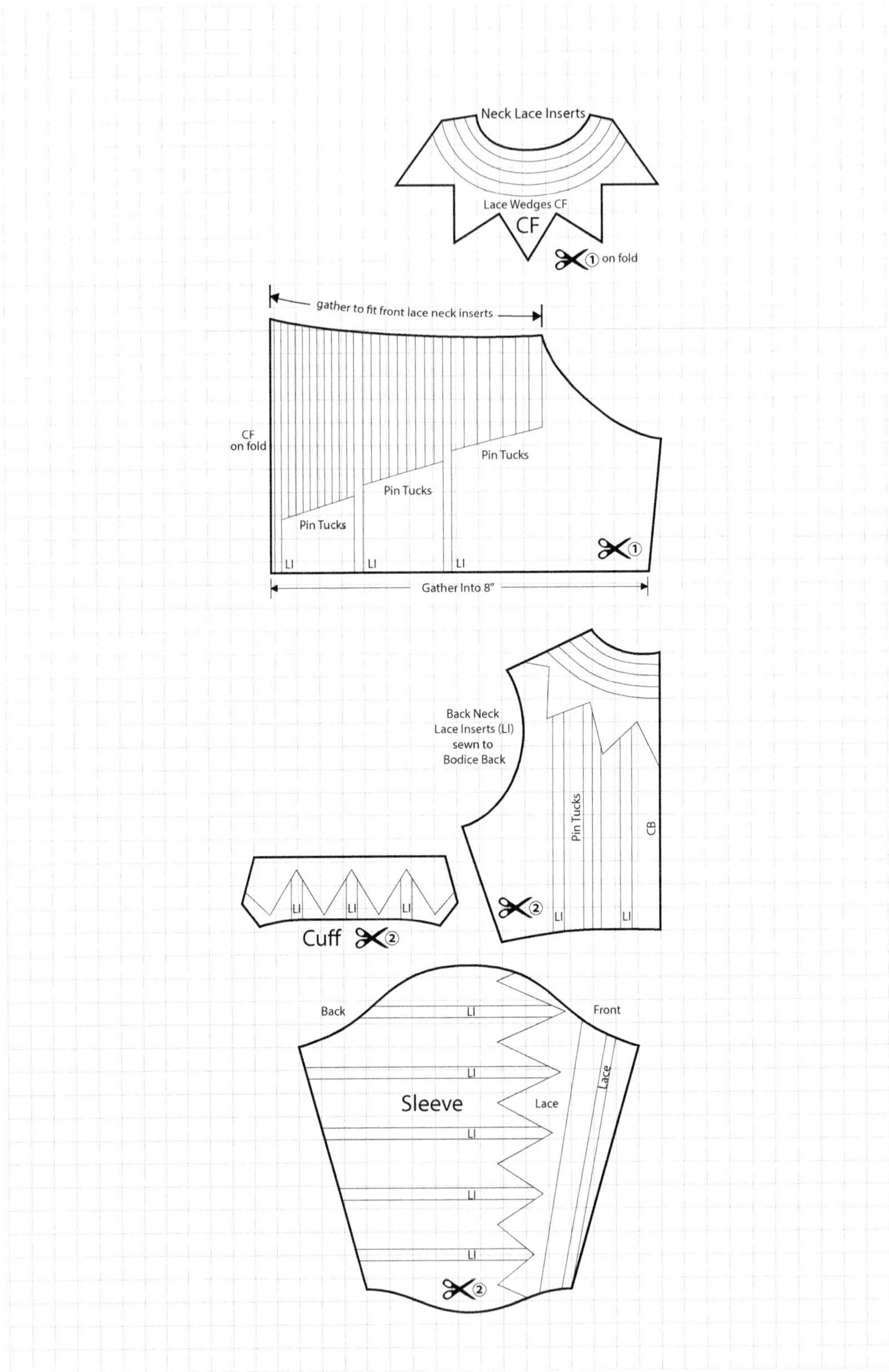
Neck Lace Inserts
Lace Wedges CF
CF
① on fold
gather to fit front lace neck inserts
CF
on fold
Pin Tucks
Pin Tucks
Pin Tucks
LI
LI
LI
①
Gather Into 8″
Back Neck
Lace Inserts (LI)
sewn to
Bodice Back
Pin Tucks
CB
②
LI
LI
LI
LI
LI
Cuff ②
Back
Front
LI
LI
Sleeve
Lace
Lace
LI
LI
LI
②

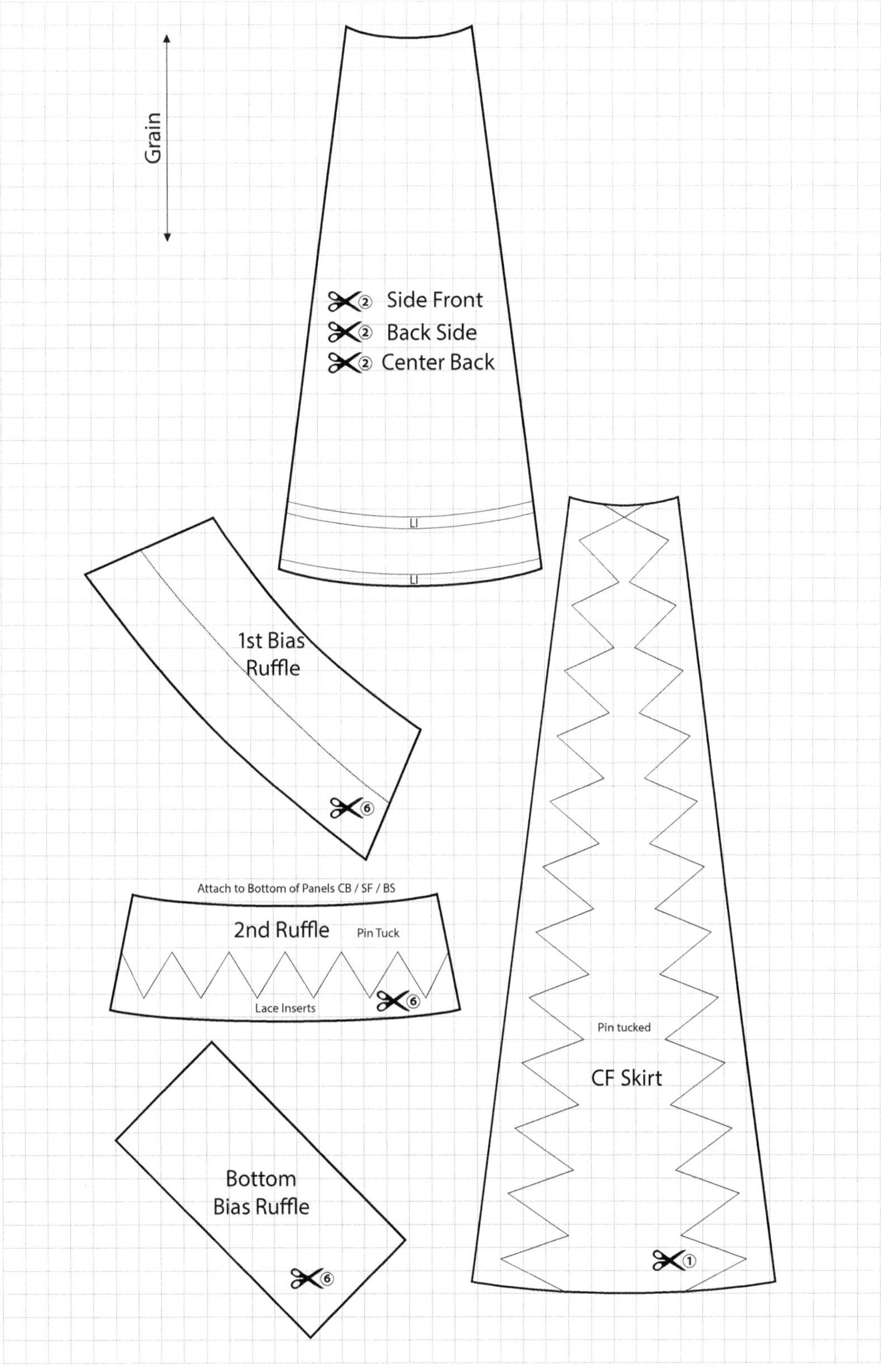
Grain
Side Front
Back Side
Center Back
LI
LI
1st Bias Ruffle
Attach to Bottom of Panels CB / SF / BS
2nd Ruffle
Pin Tuck
Lace Inserts
Bottom Bias Ruffle
Pin tucked
CF Skirt

1915

Checked Wool Suit

The First World War began with two opposing alliances: the Allies of the United Kingdom, France, and the Russian Empire, and the Central Powers of Germany, Austria-Hungary, and Italy. In 1917, the United States joined Britain in the war because Germany sank American merchant ships bound for the British Isles. By the end of the war, over 30 countries were involved and more than 9 million combatants and 7 million civilians had died. The war paved the way for major political and geographic changes and instigated a seismic shift in the role of women in society.

By 1913, many women were entering the workforce, but most middle- and upper-class women could still expect to lead a domestic life. Working-class women worked long hours, especially in the textile industry and in domestic service. With the outbreak of the Great War, everyday clothing had to adapt to reflect the lives of ordinary women in extraordinary times. Sartorial restrictions relaxed as women met the needs of jobs left behind by men.

Before the war, Paris led the world of fashion. Due to the privations of war and loss of communication between the United States and Europe, New York emerged as a fashion leader. New designs were created based on the combination

Jacket side

Jacket back

of both femininity and practicality that were essential to European women. With metal shortages and a need for physical freedom, the Great War brought about the end of the corset. By the end of the war, most fashion-conscious women were wearing the much less oppressive brassiere.

For practical purposes, the narrow tube-shaped silhouette of the early 1910s gave way to a shorter and looser skirt. Jackets and blouses became less structured. Most garments included ample pockets. Hats developed a utilitarian quality and tended to sit quite low on the forehead, covering the eyebrows. As women dressed for new roles, gender-dictated dress codes also relaxed. Women wore trousers in many occupations. Many stopped wearing jewelry. Lavish clothing became rare. Most clothing colors were dull, while black became common, as it was easier to hide dirt and was also fully appropriate for mourning dead soldiers.

This 1915 two-piece suit from the Hereford collection is a lightweight black and white checked wool and fulfilled the requirements of a woman entering the workforce. The jacket has straight two-piece sleeves finished with a 4-inch slightly flared matching cuff. The extravagance of the two-piece sleeve may have been to conserve fabric. The jacket lapels are single-peaked and decorated at the center of the lapel with small, cream floral embroidery.

The jacket has an 'A' shape that flares at the bottom just below the hip line. The waist is gently pulled in with a 2½-inch self-belt that snaps shut with two snaps under a rectangle of the suit fabric, slightly bigger than the belt. The belt rectangle also has a cream floral embroidery.

The skirt has five gored panels. The center front is cut on a fold. The tops of the skirt panels are gathered directly onto a 3-inch twill facing. The skirt closure is faced with a placket of the black and white wool and is closed with four snaps. The finished skirt length is approximately mid-calf.

Collar detail

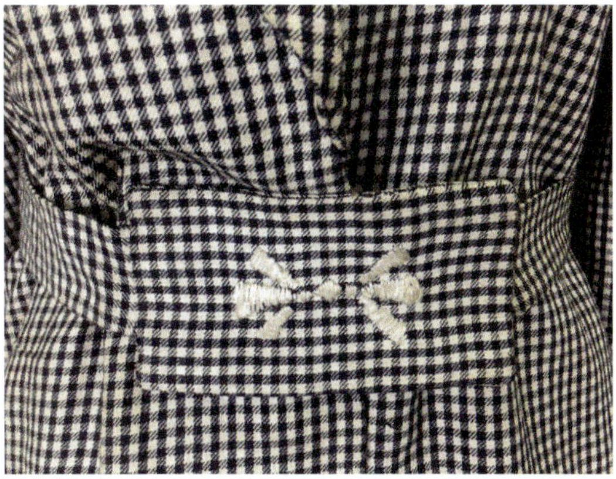

Belt detail

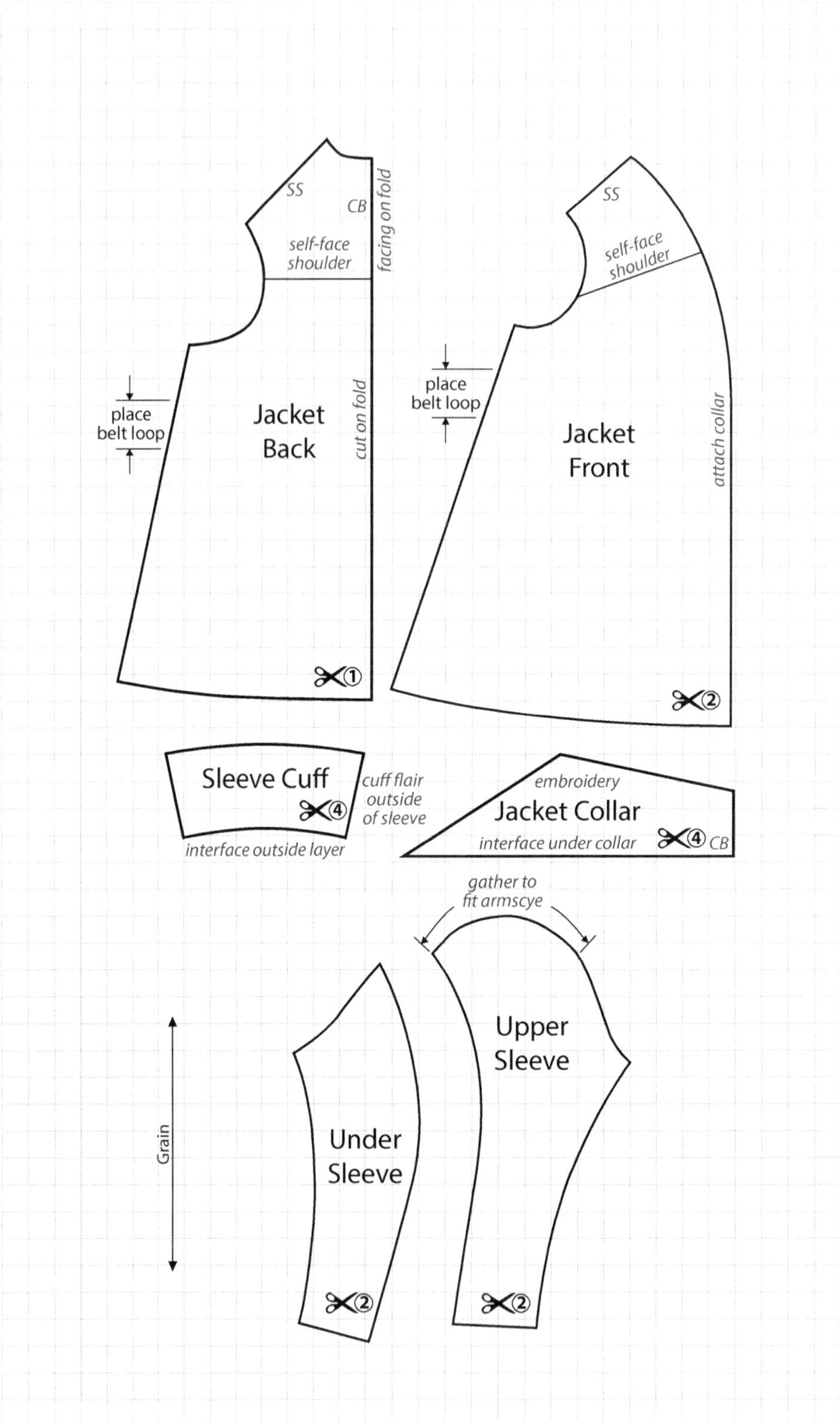
SS
CB
facing on fold
self-face shoulder
place belt loop
Jacket Back
cut on fold
①
SS
self-face shoulder
place belt loop
Jacket Front
attach collar
②
Sleeve Cuff
④
cuff flair outside of sleeve
interface outside layer
embroidery
Jacket Collar
interface under collar
④ CB
gather to fit armscye
Upper Sleeve
Grain
Under Sleeve
②
②

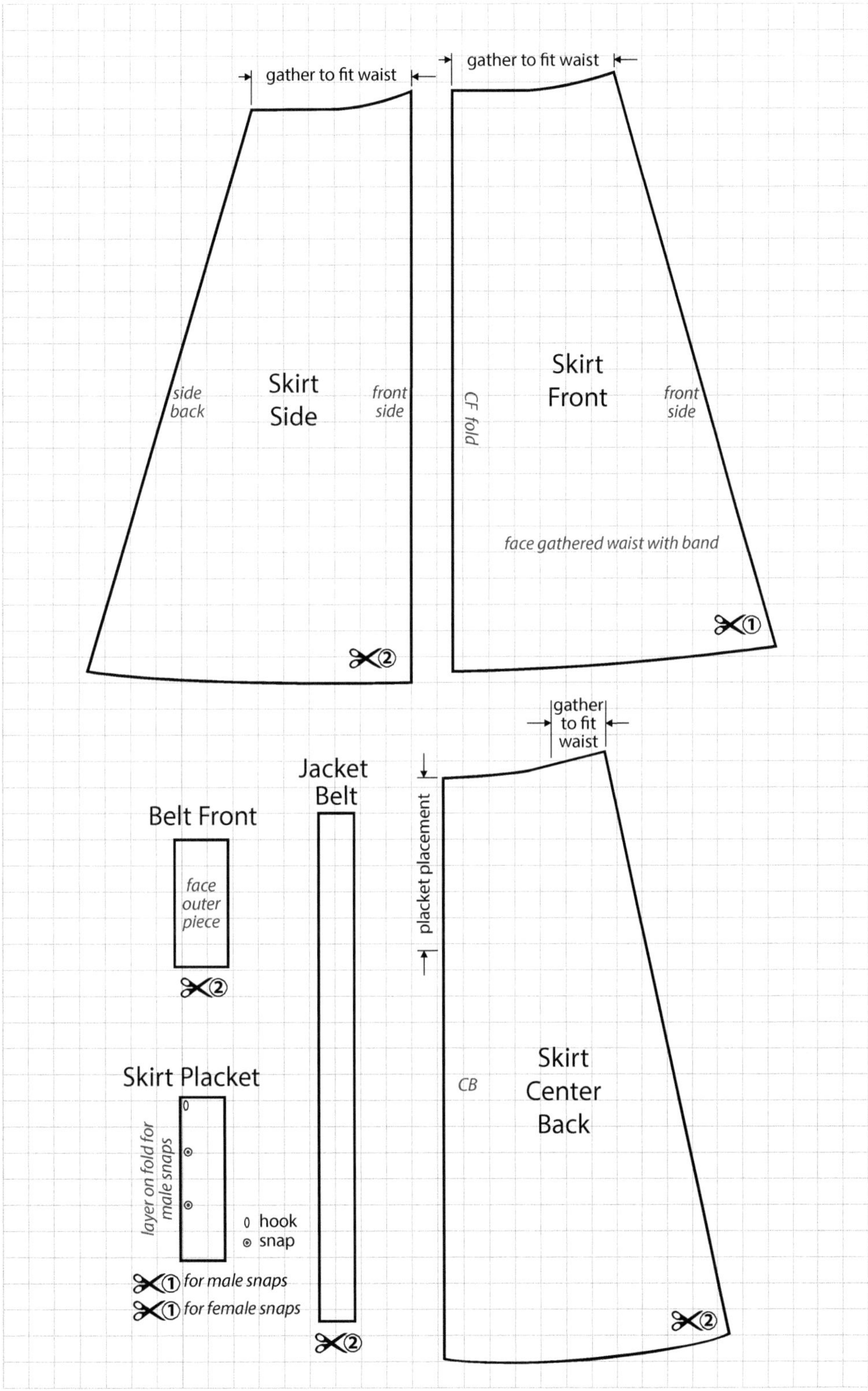
gather to fit waist
gather to fit waist
Skirt Side
side back
front side
Skirt Front
CF fold
front side
face gathered waist with band
2
1
gather to fit waist
placket placement
Jacket Belt
Belt Front
face outer piece
2
Skirt Placket
layer on fold for male snaps
hook
snap
1 for male snaps
1 for female snaps
2
Skirt Center Back
CB
2

1916

Linen Skirt and Blouse

By 1916, the Great War silhouette for women had been firmly established. This everyday dress has some interesting aspects that would have embraced war-time needs, but it also has some features which elevate it from war concerns.

This pink linen skirt and blouse epitomize the silhouette worn by women during the Great War. The torso is less restricted and the skirt is pleated and barrel-shaped. The skirt is low-calf in length. The most extraordinary aspect of the dress is its color. This bright pink is not typical. The colors of most women's garments were generally subdued browns, greys, and blacks. The pink is lively and playful, the antithesis of the nightmare of war. Perhaps it was a cheerful reminder of better times.

The bodice has a square neckline finished with a strip of self-bias. It has gathers from neck to waist across the

Bodice front

Side view of skirt and blouse

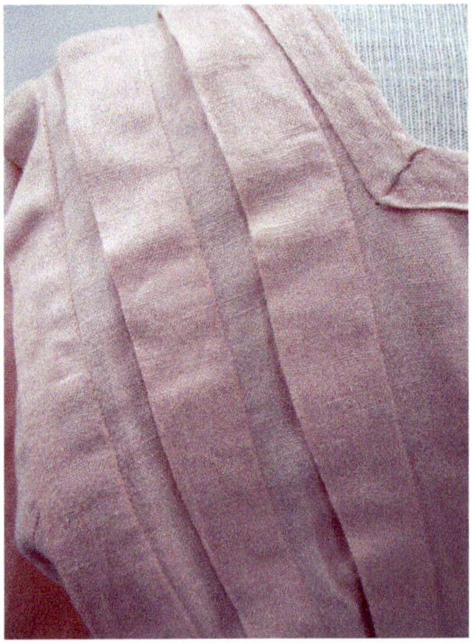

Shoulder pleats

Inside twill tape waistband at skirt front closure

front. There are also pleats that go from the waist up over the shoulders and down to the waist in the back. The blouse opens on the left side under the fold that runs over the shoulder. The straight ¾-length sleeves are finished with 1½-inch cuffs. The bottom of the blouse is finished and tucked into an inside twill tape waistband.

The skirt is full and gathered at the waist. A front seam runs down the skirt and jogs over toward the skirt center and finishes at the hem. The top edge of the skirt is folded over and securely sewed into an inside waistband. The blouse is tucked into the skirt and held down with several sets of snaps, hooks, and eyes.

Skirt back gather

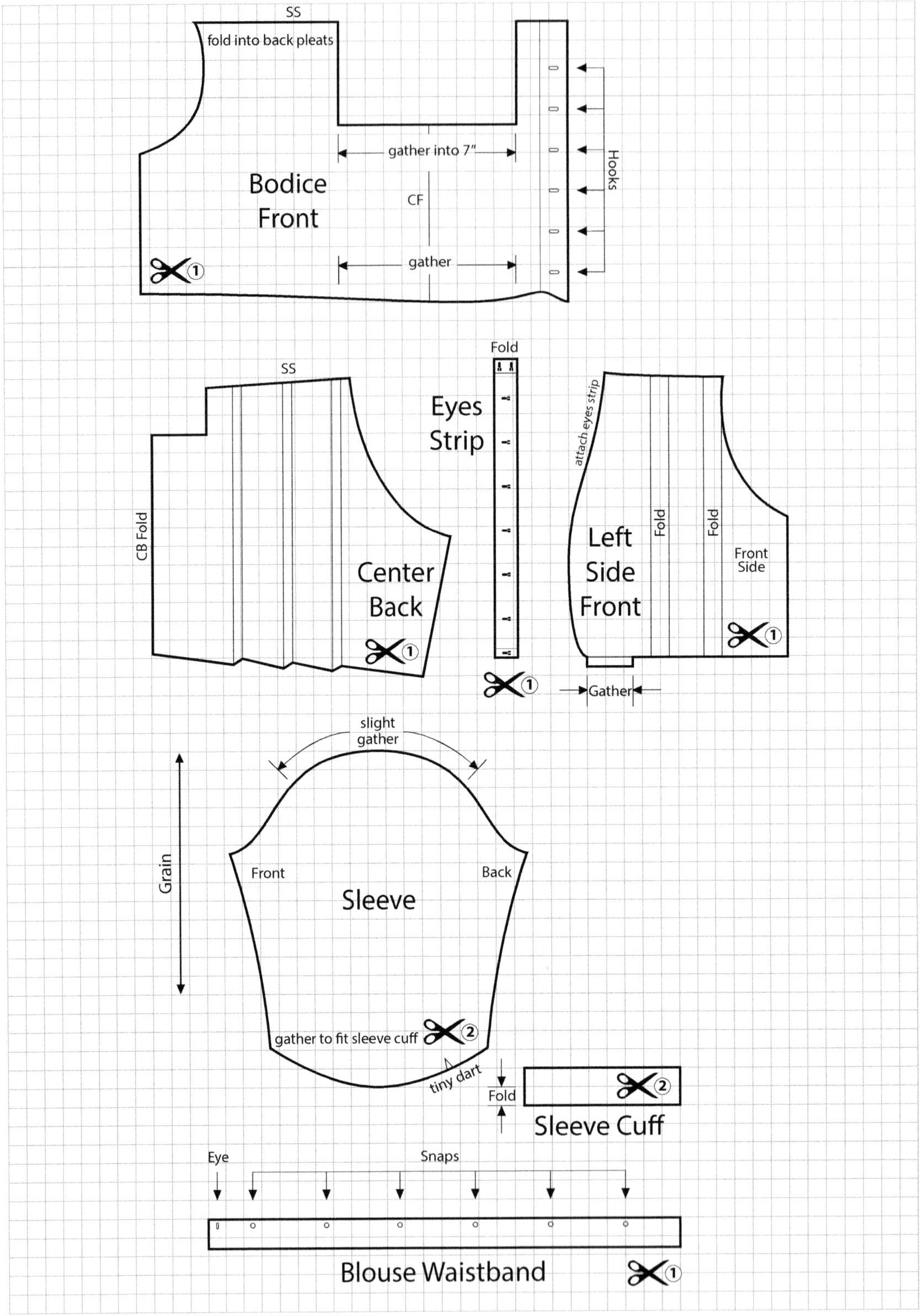
SS
fold into back pleats
gather into 7"
Hooks
Bodice Front
CF
gather
1
Fold
SS
Eyes Strip
attach eyes strip
CB Fold
Center Back
1
Left Side Front
Fold
Fold
Front Side
1
1
Gather
slight gather
Grain
Front
Back
Sleeve
gather to fit sleeve cuff
2
tiny dart
Fold
2
Sleeve Cuff
Eye
Snaps
Blouse Waistband
1

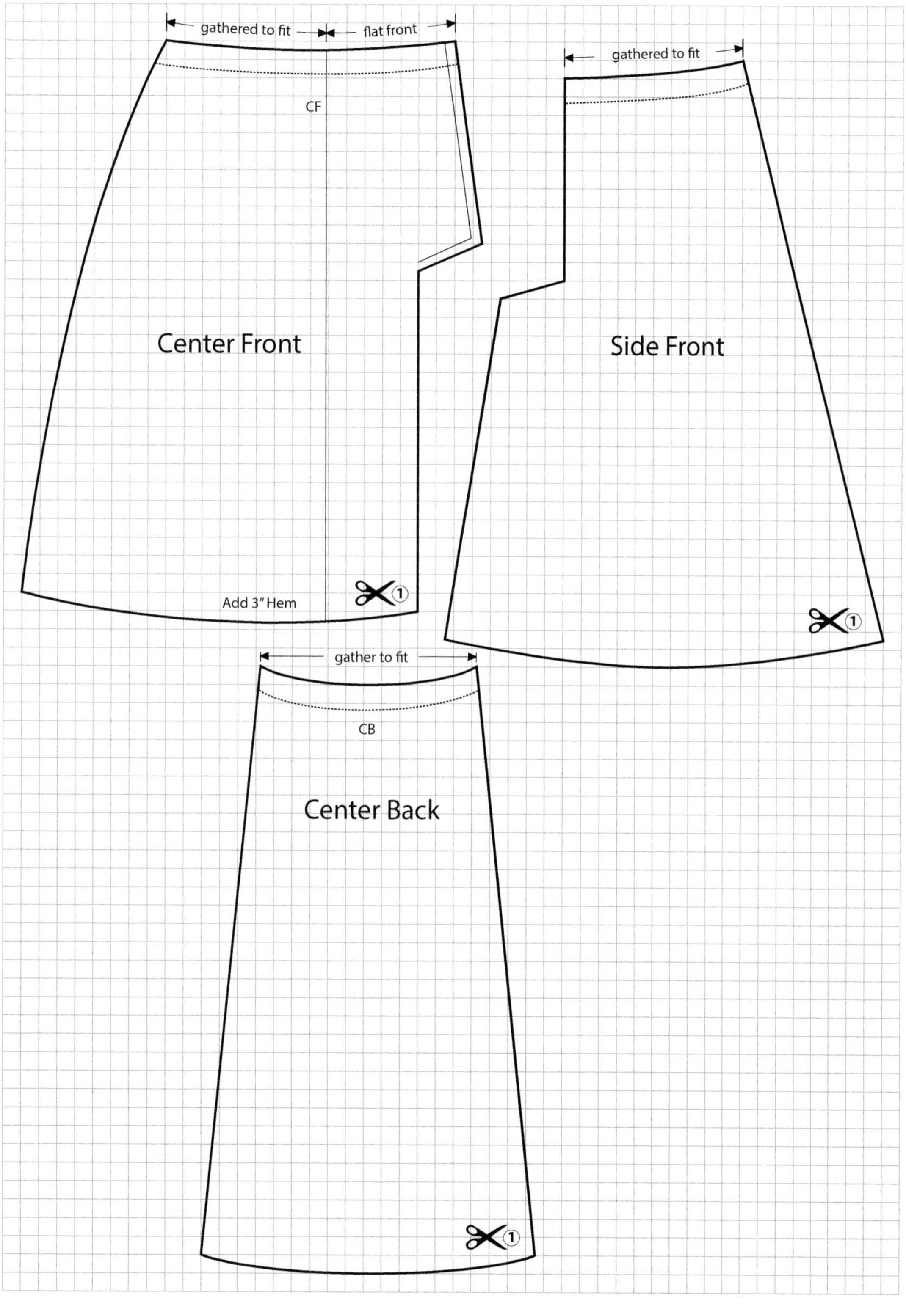
gathered to fit
flat front
CF
Center Front
Add 3" Hem
gathered to fit
Side Front
gather to fit
CB
Center Back

1924

Silk Drop Waist Evening Dress

The 1920s, before the stock market crash, were characterized by prosperity and independence that were a radical change for women.

By 1924, the new design seen in this gown was influenced by social changes and new technology. After the war women continued to develop footholds in a large variety of new areas of employment. The men who returned from the war found many women less concerned with traditional hearth and home. Women answered to themselves rather than to a father, husband or brother. A woman could be a financial partner rather than a financial burden and women played a greater role outside of the home. They led freer lives. The strict confines of the Victorian and Edwardian eras were firmly left behind with their mothers and grandmothers.

The ideal modern silhouette became the slim lines of a young girl or even a young boy. The bust was reduced and the waist and bottom flattened into a cylinder. Even the long Edwardian styling of hair was bobbed into a simple childlike cut. Ideal matronly curves were replaced with the silhouette of youth. This was seen as a fresh start.

In keeping with these sweeping changes, this charmingly simple drop waist was a refreshing new fashion. The

Back of dress

Skirt flared out

Tiny corded bias piping at waist

dress is so small and so narrow that when I photographed it, I could not find a female mannequin for it in the museum. "Female curves" were a hindrance. I finally photographed this frock on a small boy's mannequin. I find this interesting and a somewhat ironic.

The information available in the museum about this garment refers to the fiber content as artificial silk. By 1924 artificial silk became known as rayon. Rayon was the first material to fall under a "semi-synthetic" category. It originates from cellulose materials such as wood pulp that undergo a chemical process in production. It is extruded in one very long filament. It was accidently invented in 1846 when chemists were working to improved explosives. Instead, they created a new fabric.

The gown is sleeveless and the shoulders and neckline is constructed of cotton net. Where the bust would be is outlined with a zigzag of two rows of gathered net sewed on top of narrow bias strips.

The gathered net appears only at the front of the bodice. The straight bodice ends at the hip, where the net skirt flairs out to a full circle.

The shoulders and neckline of the tank top-shaped bodice is constructed of cotton net. Where the bust would be is outlined with a zigzag of two rows of gathered net sewn on top of narrow bias strips. The gathered net only appears on the front of the bodice.

The straight tank ends at the hip, where the net skirt flairs out to a full circle. The skirt is comprised of nine rows of graduating sized bias-cut ribbons of the artificial silk. The armscyes are finished with tiny pink bias and the top of the skirt is piped with the same pink bias strips. The back of the V-neck gown is filled with a panel of pink net. At the bottom of the back V-neck is a large, droopy bow with tails that trail down the back to mid-skirt. The gown opens along the left side from under arm to hip. It closes with seven small snaps hidden in the side seam.

Gathered net attached to bodice

Snaps hidden in the left side seam

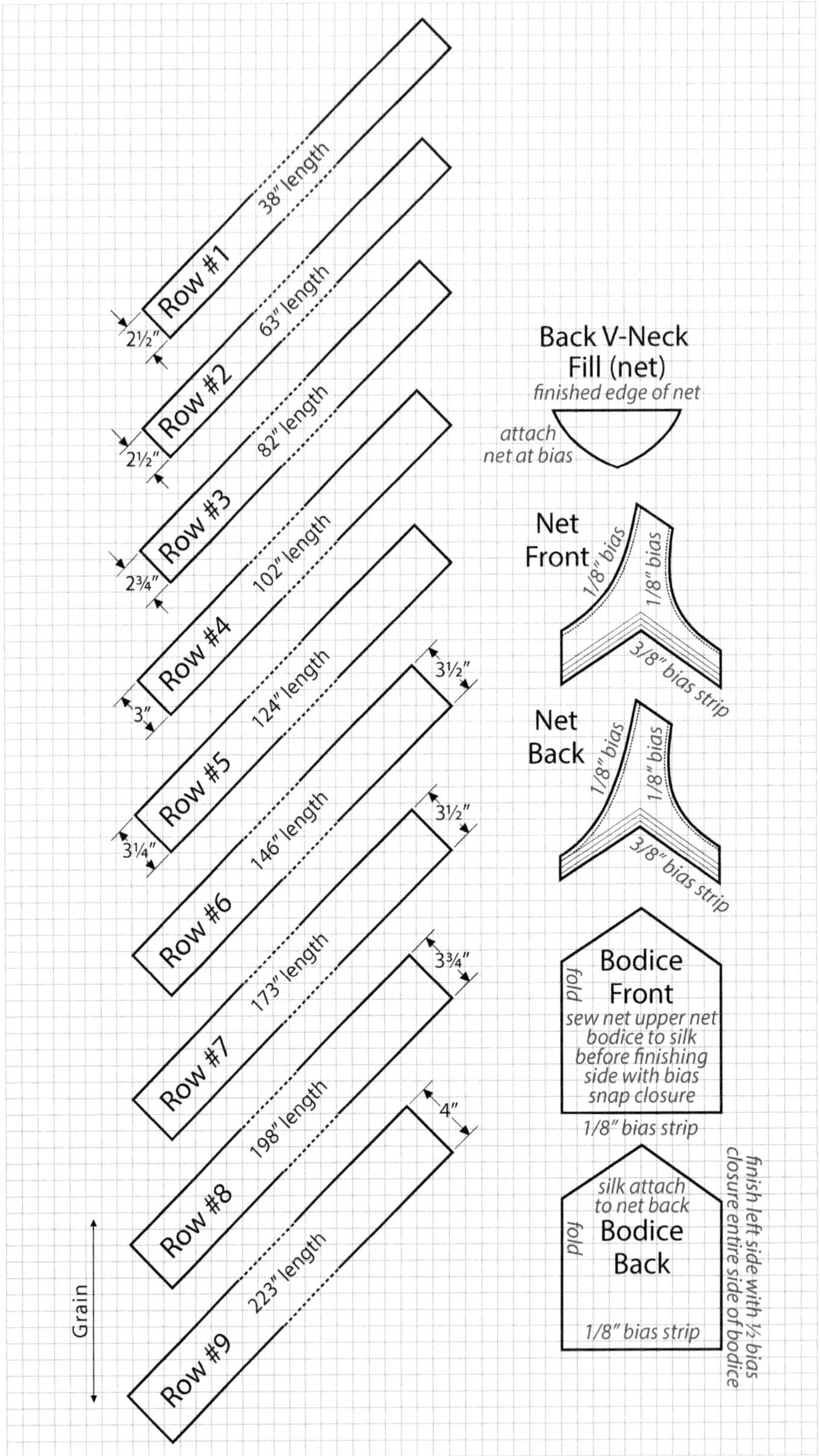
Row #1
38″ length
2½″
Row #2
63″ length
2½″
Row #3
82″ length
2¾″
Row #4
102″ length
3″
Row #5
124″ length
3½″
3¼″
Row #6
146″ length
3½″
Row #7
173″ length
3¾″
Row #8
198″ length
4″
Row #9
223″ length
Grain
Back V-Neck Fill (net)
finished edge of net
attach net at bias
Net Front
1/8″ bias
1/8″ bias
3/8″ bias strip
Net Back
1/8″ bias
1/8″ bias
3/8″ bias strip
Bodice Front
fold
sew net upper net bodice to silk before finishing side with bias snap closure
1/8″ bias strip
silk attach to net back
Bodice Back
fold
1/8″ bias strip
finish left side with ½ bias closure entire side of bodice

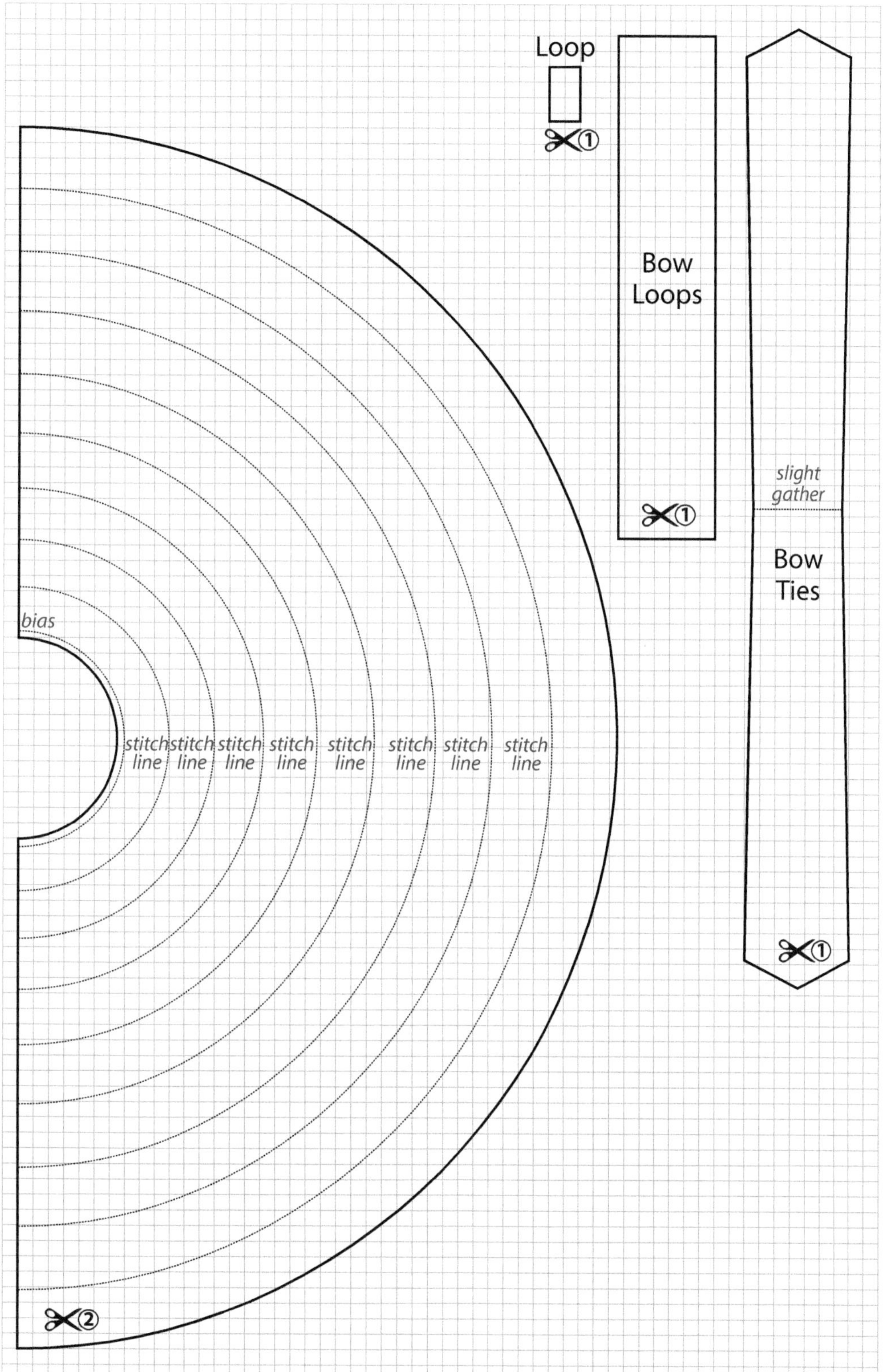
Loop
Bow Loops
Bow Ties
slight gather
bias
stitch line
stitch line
stitch line
stitch line
stitch line
stitch line
stitch line
stitch line

1924

Striped Drop Waist Silk Dress

In 1918, at the end of the First World War, British women who owned property and were over the age of 30 got the right to vote. All British women over 21 won the right in 1928. In 1920, the Nineteenth Amendment to the U.S. Constitution was ratified and granted all American women the right to vote.

In Britain, 8 million men did not return home from the war and millions more were badly injured. This left an entire generation of young women without enough husbands to go around. Young women knew that life was short and could end at any moment. This was an age of emancipation and a blurring of class lines. The women, who became known as flappers, wanted to enjoy life to its fullest and fastest.

By the mid 1920s, the flapper had a distinct look. Her hair was bobbed short and skirts ended at the knee. The hosiery industry flourished. The popular dances encouraged the stomping and kicking of exposed legs. High heels emphasized their calfs and allowed a swing of their backsides when they walked. Flappers chose activities to please themselves, not a father or a husband.

Collar back

6-inch skirt side pleat

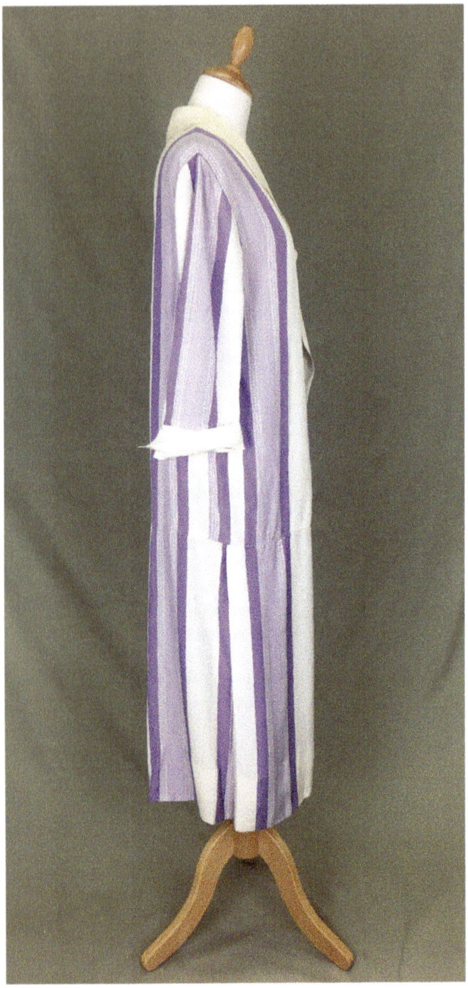

Side profile

The cosmetics industry grew as women used bold makeup. In 1922, Howard Carter discovered King Tutankhamun's tomb. Egypt mania became part of popular culture. Many women lined their eyes with dark kohl similar to the Egyptian images.

Geometric Art Deco styling reflected the modern streamline attitude. Women tried to look younger by wearing clothes that didn't emphasize their curves. Women bound their chests, giving themselves an androgenized appearance. Chinoiserie was a popular exotic style, from the simple straight lines of the kimono coat to the popularity of Mahjong tournaments. The simple straight style lines were more economical than the numerous yards of fabric needed for clothing of the previous generation. Dresses were also easier to construct, and in that regard, more democratic. The ideal woman was youthful and energetic, a far cry from the mono-bosomed matron of 20 years before.

This silk frock from 1924 reflects the geometric lines of the Art Deco style. This dress is straight from shoulder to hem, reinforced with the bold vertical stripes. The neckline has an overlapping surplus front, much like the fashionable kimono style. It is finished with a cream-colored silk shawl collar.

The back of this dress has almost the same style lines as the front. The fabric stripes make straight lines from shoulder to hip and continue through the waistline to the hem. The ¾-length sleeves are set into the armscye with no fullness. They end with cream-colored silk cuffs that match the collar.

Both sides of the skirt have 6-inch deep knife pleats. The pleats allow an ample stride but maintain the straight vertical stripe lines. The skirt waist sits at the high hip. The stripes from shoulder to hem are perfectly matched at the waist. The skirt ends just below the knee.

Inside French seam

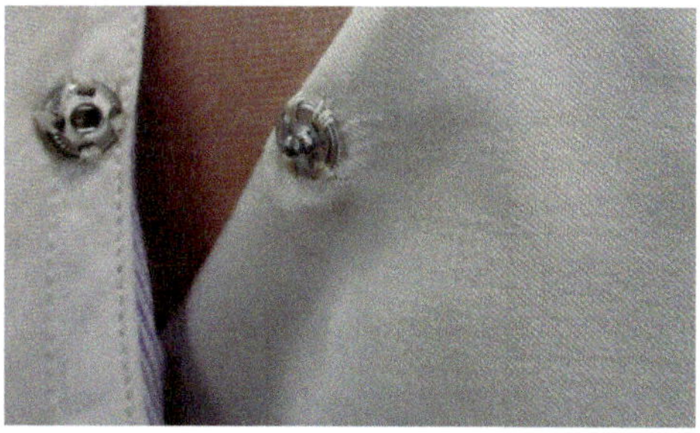

Blouse snap

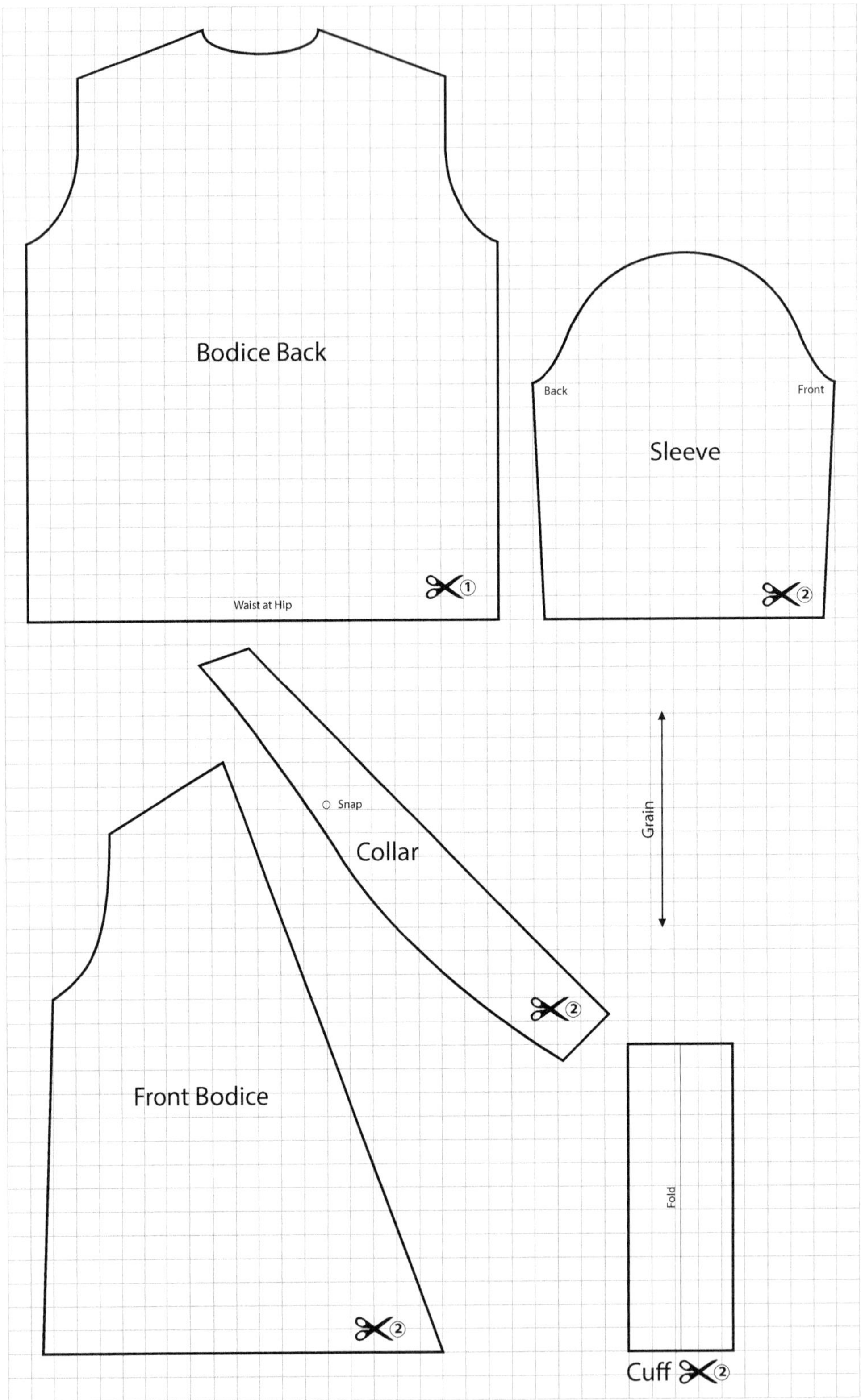
Bodice Back
Waist at Hip
Back
Front
Sleeve
Snap
Collar
Grain
Front Bodice
Fold
Cuff

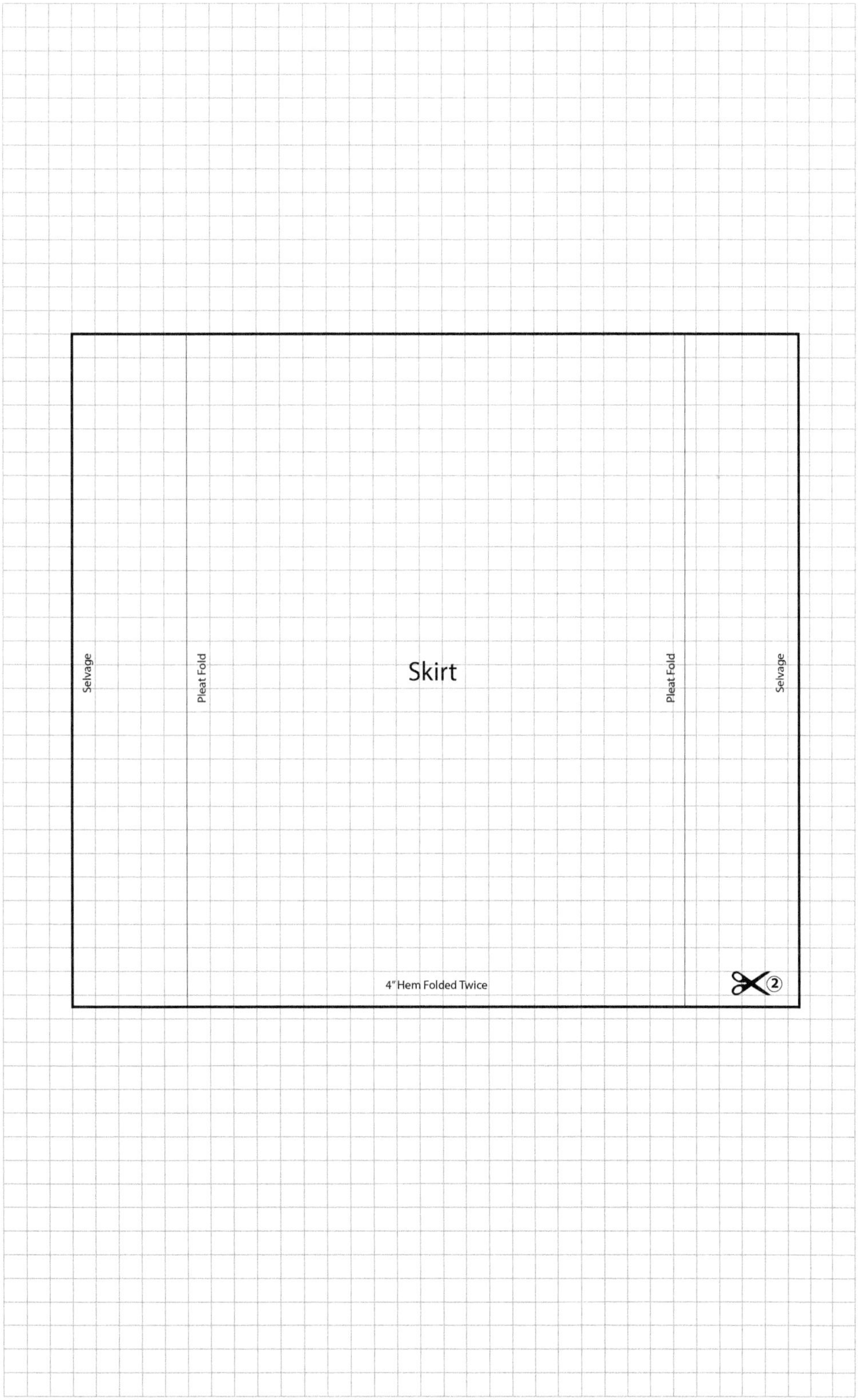
Selvage
Pleat Fold
Skirt
Pleat Fold
Selvage
4" Hem Folded Twice
2

1933

Velvet Bias Gown

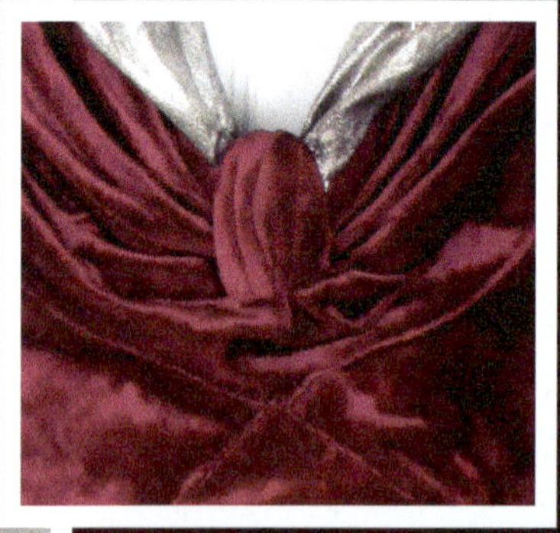

In October 1929, the Wall Street Crash plunged the U.S. into an economic depression which affected many millions of people throughout the Western world for almost a full decade. Politically, the 1930s was unstable, filled with revolutions, dictatorships, invasions, and the weakening of the League of Nations. The Japanese invaded Manchuria; the monarchy was overthrown in Spain; Hitler came to power in Germany.

In the U.S., the arts were supported by the patronage of the Government and a few wealthy citizens but economic privation made artistic expression even more difficult. The Art Deco style adapted to these advances with more curved lines in furniture, interiors, and clothing. This ideal world looked like a slick, polished, modern streamlined machine. This was a period of visual austerity and simplicity which lasted until just before the Second World War broke out. Paris was still the center of the Art Deco world but London and New York were not far behind.

During the Depression, one indulgence that many people could manage was going to movies. It was an

Gown side

Back of gown

escape from the heartache of the world. Hollywood became a major source of style in clothing, interiors, and artifacts. Actresses like Greta Garbo and Marlene Dietrich served as role models for women hungry for glamour.

The stylish evening gowns of the early 1930s showed both lean and curvy silhouettes. The flat chested flapper of the 1920s was replaced with a more traditional female shape. The waistline reappeared.

In France during the late 1920s, Madeline Vionette was one of the most influential clothing designers. She was famous for her excellent technique with bias cutting of fabric that molded to the body. By the 1930s, her expertise in bias cut gave a sinuous, curvaceous, and elegant line to long evening gowns.

This 1933 burgundy velvet bias-cut floor length gown appears simple. Its simplicity is deceptive. It is carefully cut on the exact bias to achieve a figure-hugging shape. The bodice front is finished straight across the collarbone with a 2-inch-wide bias panel of silver metallic fabric. The square neckline is created with the 2-inch-wide velvet straps that go over the shoulders that become part of the back of the dress. The front edge of the straps display two large decorative white crystal buttons.

The bottom of the bodice is cut with wedges, short in the front, long in the back. Those wedges fit into the opposite wedges cut down into the skirt front and back. The most elaborate area of the gown is the back. It has a plunging opening that goes three-quarters down. The back-opening has fullness at the base that finishes in soft pleats centered with a large burgundy velvet rosette. The back-opening is faced with the silver metallic fabric.

Gown back with rosette

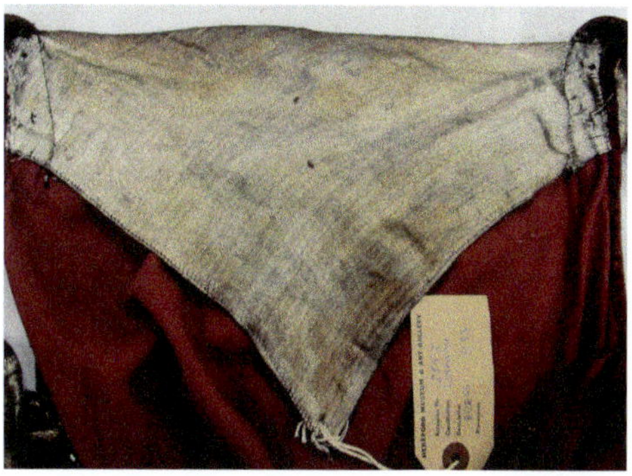

Inside metallic fabric

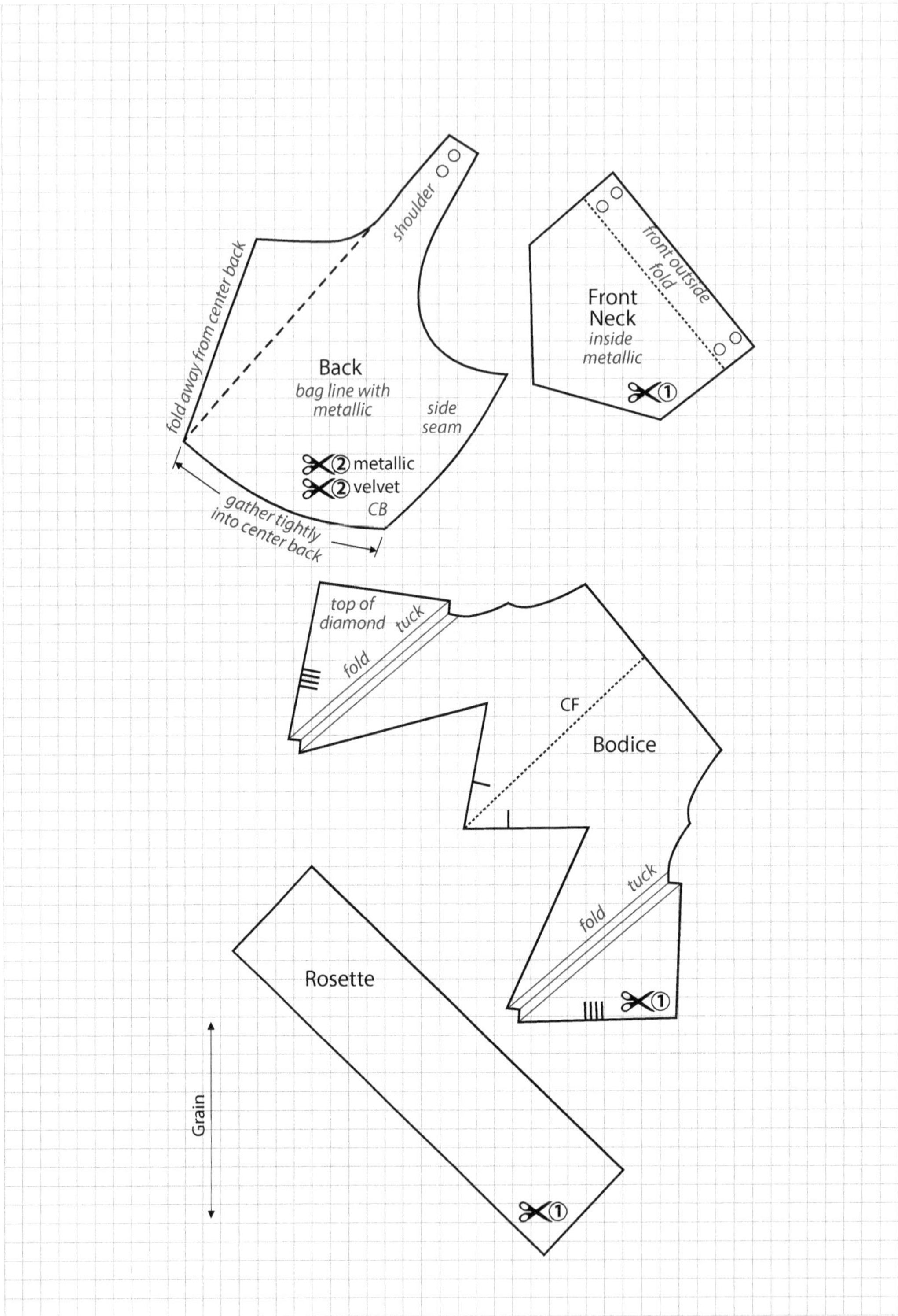
shoulder
fold away from center back
Back
bag line with metallic
side seam
2 metallic
2 velvet
CB
gather tightly into center back
front outside fold
Front Neck
inside metallic
1
top of diamond
tuck
fold
CF
Bodice
tuck
fold
1
Rosette
Grain
1

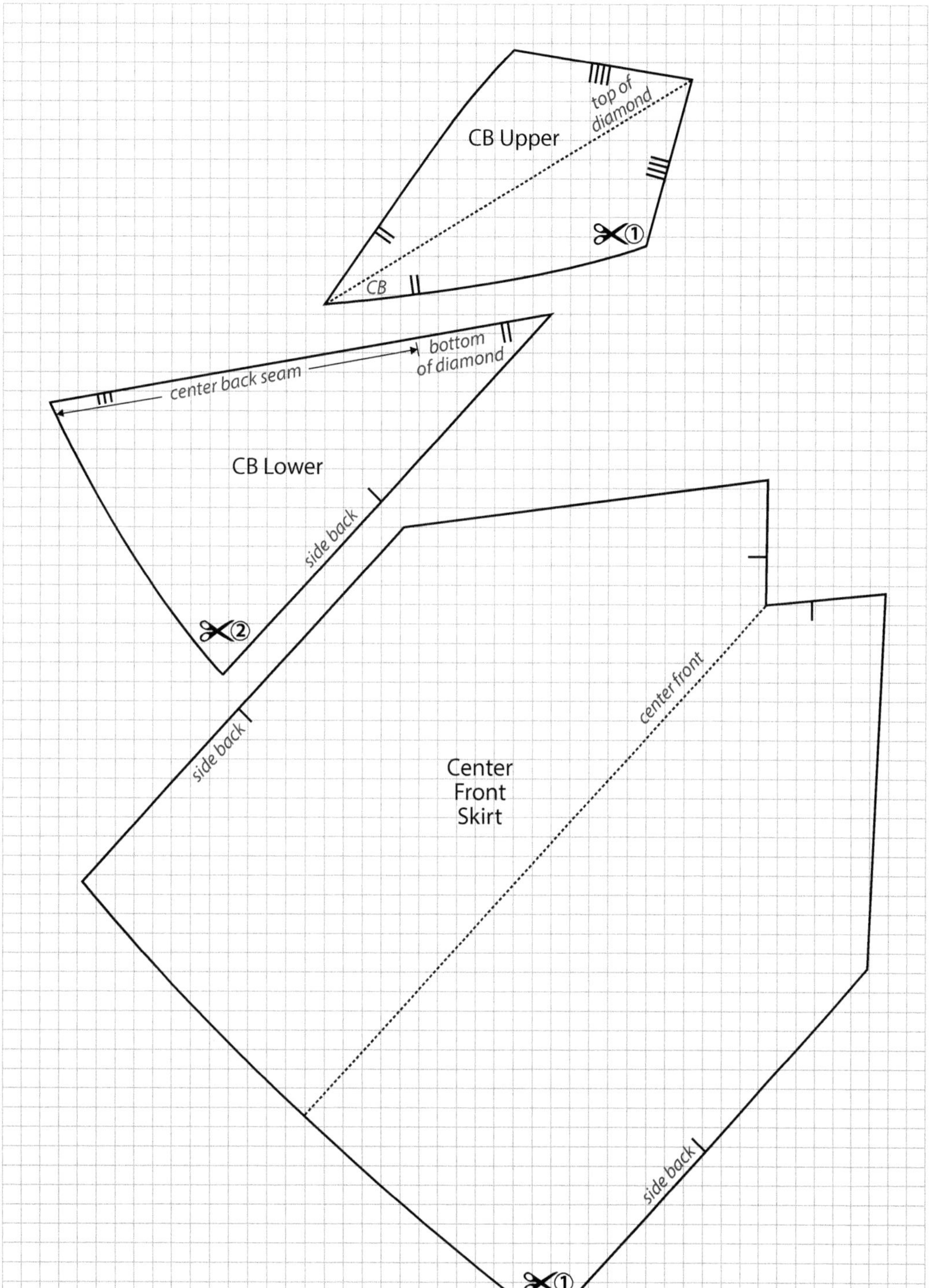

CB Upper
top of diamond
CB
①
center back seam
bottom of diamond
CB Lower
side back
②
Center Front Skirt
center front
side back
side back
①

1936

Wool Dress and Cape

The Great Depression affected economies worldwide. After 1929, the U.S. economy crashed and the banks called in millions of dollars of First World War European loans. In the U.S., 24 percent of the population was unemployed. In the U.K., over 20 percent of the workforce was unemployed and in Germany, unemployment reached nearly 30 percent. Rural areas and heavy industry suffered the most. Worst hit was the heavy industry in Northern Ireland, Scotland, Wales, and the north of England. Industries were already struggling because they had not modernized after the war and had been badly affected by competition from other countries. With the Depression, entire industries crumbled.

American industrial cities also suffered badly. American cities that relied on service industries fared better. To make matters worse, much of the U.S. lower Midwestern states suffered the worst droughts in history which led to the Dust Bowl years. Thirty-three mile per hour winds formed and stripped the topsoil from the drought-affected farms in the Midwest, forcing a huge American migration from the Midwest to the West Coast.

Cape yoke and knife pleats

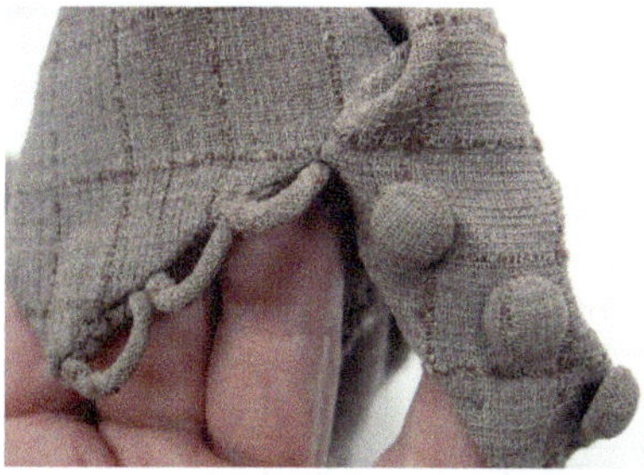

Sleeve covered buttons and loops

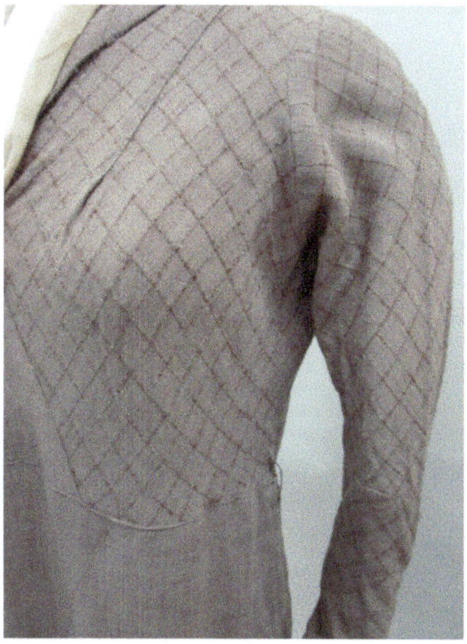

Side front bodice and sleeve

Cape side

Cape laid flat

Innovations of Coco Chanel and Elsa Schiaparelli continued the tendency toward the disappearance of class distinction in women's daytime clothes. Women of all classes became engaged in some sort of work, and therefore a kind of working uniform evolved.

In 1936, this stylish dress could be worn during the day and adding the matching cape quickly and easily turned it into an evening dress. This mushroom-colored dress had an Art Deco influenced asymmetrical pleated collar, a pleated insert at the skirt center and a matching pleated cape.

The two primary fabrics used in the dress and cape are a solid and checkered print georgette. The checkered fabric is used on the bodice, sleeves, and part of the cape. An isosceles triangle of solid fabric sits over the center of both the front and back bodice. The asymmetrical collar is comprised of two layers. The under layer is a small knife-pleated mushroom georgette fabric and the over layer is a knife pleated cream silk chiffon. The entire neckline is finished with a soft roll of cream chiffon. It has long sleeves that close at the wrist with four matching fabric buttons and loops.

The skirt is made from solid fabric. At the top front and back of the skirt is an inverted isosceles triangle, also of solid fabric. The skirt is flared with a gore shaped insert, of knife-pleated solid fabric at the center front hem. The soft waistline is emphasized with a belt covered with the same fabric. An 8-inch side seam opening is closed with snaps. The skirt is low calf length. The skirt front knife-pleated godet gives an interesting clean line yet provides a comfortable stride.

The elbow-length cape is made from shoulder and side panels of the checkered fabric. The two flared pieces of the cape are made from the knife-pleated solid fabric and end well below the elbows.

Dress with cape

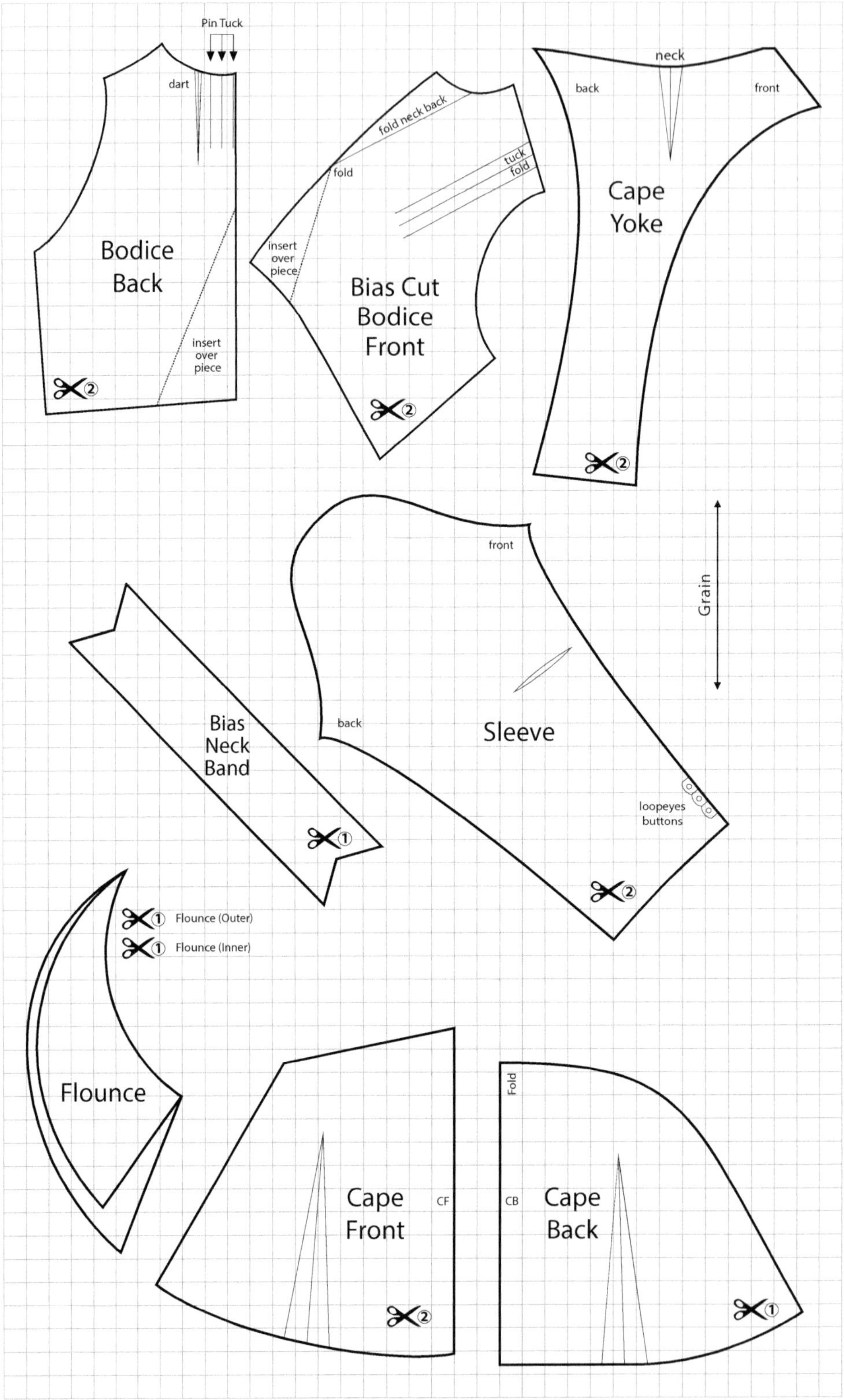
Pin Tuck
dart
Bodice Back
insert over piece
fold neck back
fold
tuck
fold
insert over piece
Bias Cut Bodice Front
neck
back
front
Cape Yoke
front
Grain
Bias Neck Band
back
Sleeve
loopeyes buttons
Flounce (Outer)
Flounce (Inner)
Flounce
Cape Front
CF
Fold
CB
Cape Back

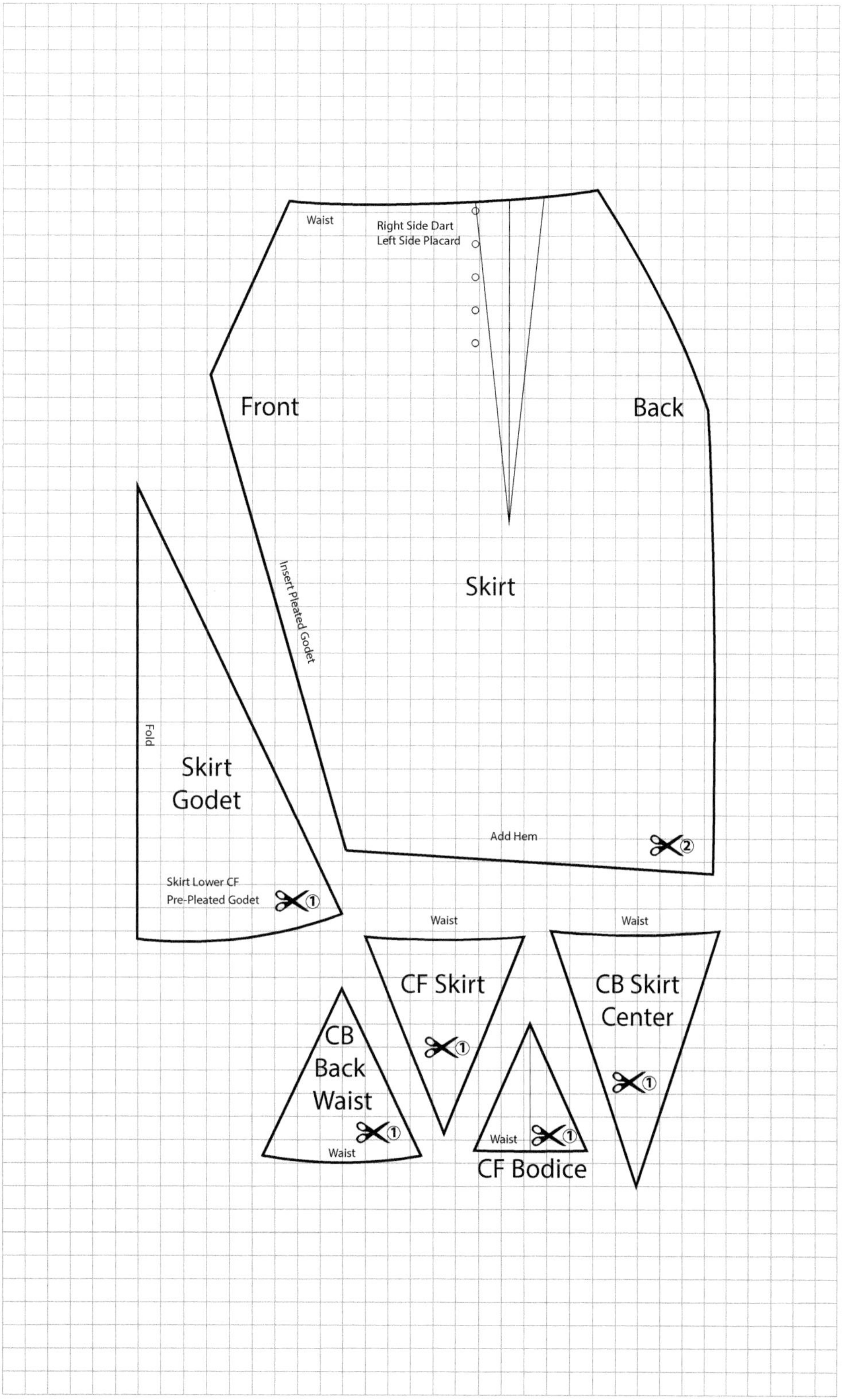
Waist
Right Side Dart
Left Side Placard
Front
Back
Skirt
Insert Pleated Godet
Add Hem
②
Fold
Skirt
Godet
Skirt Lower CF
Pre-Pleated Godet
①
Waist
CF Skirt
①
Waist
CB Skirt
Center
①
CB
Back
Waist
①
Waist
Waist
①
CF Bodice

1945

Rayon Crepe Utility Dress

On September 3, 1939, the United Kingdom declared war on Germany. In 1941, the United States declared war on Japan and by 1945, 101 countries were involved. There were extensive shortages of wool, silk, leather, rubber, metal, and cotton. All of which had an impact on fashion. Raw materials and manufactured goods were channeled into the war effort. Heavy restrictions were placed on the making of civilian clothing.

Women's clothing shortened from the mid-calf skirts of the 1930s to just below the knee. Shoulders took on a boxy military silhouette and women's suit jackets resembled uniforms. In England in 1941, the British Board of Trade introduced the regulations for "Utility Clothes." Every civilian was issued 20 coupons biannually and each garment was valued at a given number of coupons. All manufacturers were forbidden to use more than a stated amount of material for any model and no clothing manufacturer was permitted to create any more than 50 styles during the year. All utility items were marked with a CC41 label which stood for "Controlled Commodity 1941." This label was used on clothing, shoes, and household furniture.

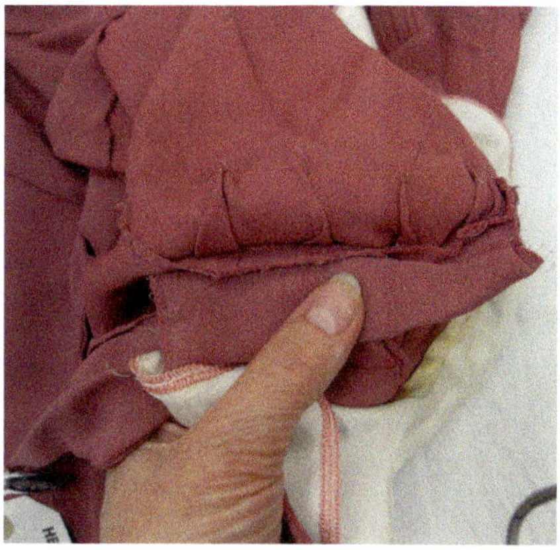

Built-in shoulder pads

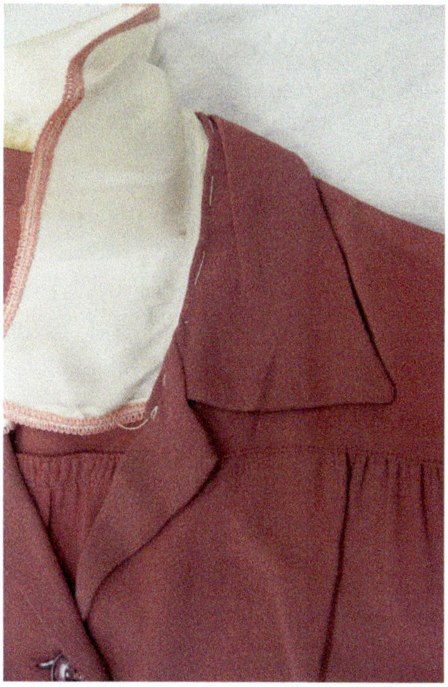

Additional white collar basted on

CC41 limits for women required no more than 2¾ yards for an overcoat (depending of the width of fabric), 2½ yards for a suit and 2 yards for a dress. Further restrictions included: no trim, fancy stitching or lace on women's underwear, no metal bones or elastic on corsets or girdles. There were no metal zippers, metal jewelry, or metal buttons. Skirts and dresses originally were limited to three buttons, six seams, two pleats and one pocket.

Similar to CC41 was the United States War Production Board LO-85 (Limited Order 85). This was the ordinance that reduced the use of textiles and labor by 15 percent. United States manufacturers were restricted in their use of materials, with possible penalties of fines or imprisonment. Clothing was carefully measured during production. Blouses and dresses could only have decorative style lines on the front of a garment. There were no big sleeves, no all-around pleats, no wide belts, and no hoods. If tucking or pleating was on a garment then ruffling could not be used and vice versa. Coats could have no swing backs, no Norfolk style backs and no epaulets on the shoulders. Americans were limited to three pairs of leather shoes a year, whereas non-leather shoes were non-rationed.

The U.K. government gave out Make Do and Mend pamphlets that encouraged women to recycle and mend everything they owned. They even gave instructions how to take apart a man's suit and make it into a woman's suit or clothing for children.

The British government encouraged women to look their best. The thought was to encourage women to maintain a positive attitude, give the men in uniform something to look forward to, and thumb their noses at the enemy.

With fabric restrictions many women's garments were made from rayon. Rayon is manufactured from regenerated cellulose fiber, frequently made from wood pulp. During the war, many fabrics were replaced with rayon. It was a fabric that could imitate wool, silk, linen, or cotton.

Toward the end of the war, when the tide began to turn for the Allies, some clothing restrictions began to relax. This dress from 1945 shows the beginning of the relaxation of tight restrictions. This 1945 dress has five buttons rather than the 1942 limitation of three buttons. It does maintain the short sleeves, square shoulders, fitted waist, and knee-length skirt typical of the war years. The rayon crepe was a common replacement fabric during war shortages on both sides of the Atlantic.

This 1945 cheerful rose-colored rayon crepe day dress has a CC41 label in the neck seam. The bodice and skirt closes at the center front with five buttons and an opening in the left side. The neck is finished with a small pointed collar. The bodice has a small yoke front and back. There is slight fullness in the bodice back that eases into the waist and the shoulder yoke. In keeping with resource restrictions, there is no interfacing in the center front panel that would normally be there to reinforce the buttonholes and button pieces.

The sleeves end just above the elbow, with four small darts creating fullness at the shoulder cap. Matching shoulder pads are sewn into the sleeve cap seam. The skirt has two box pleats in the front. The back panels are all slightly gored. This dress has a white collar that is trimmed with pink edging and matching cuffs. The white collar and cuffs were added later and loosely tacked on with a running stitch. There was also a zipper in the side closure that does not appear to be part of the original dress, as the zipper and dress do not match. Originally, the dress may have closed with snaps.

Dress side

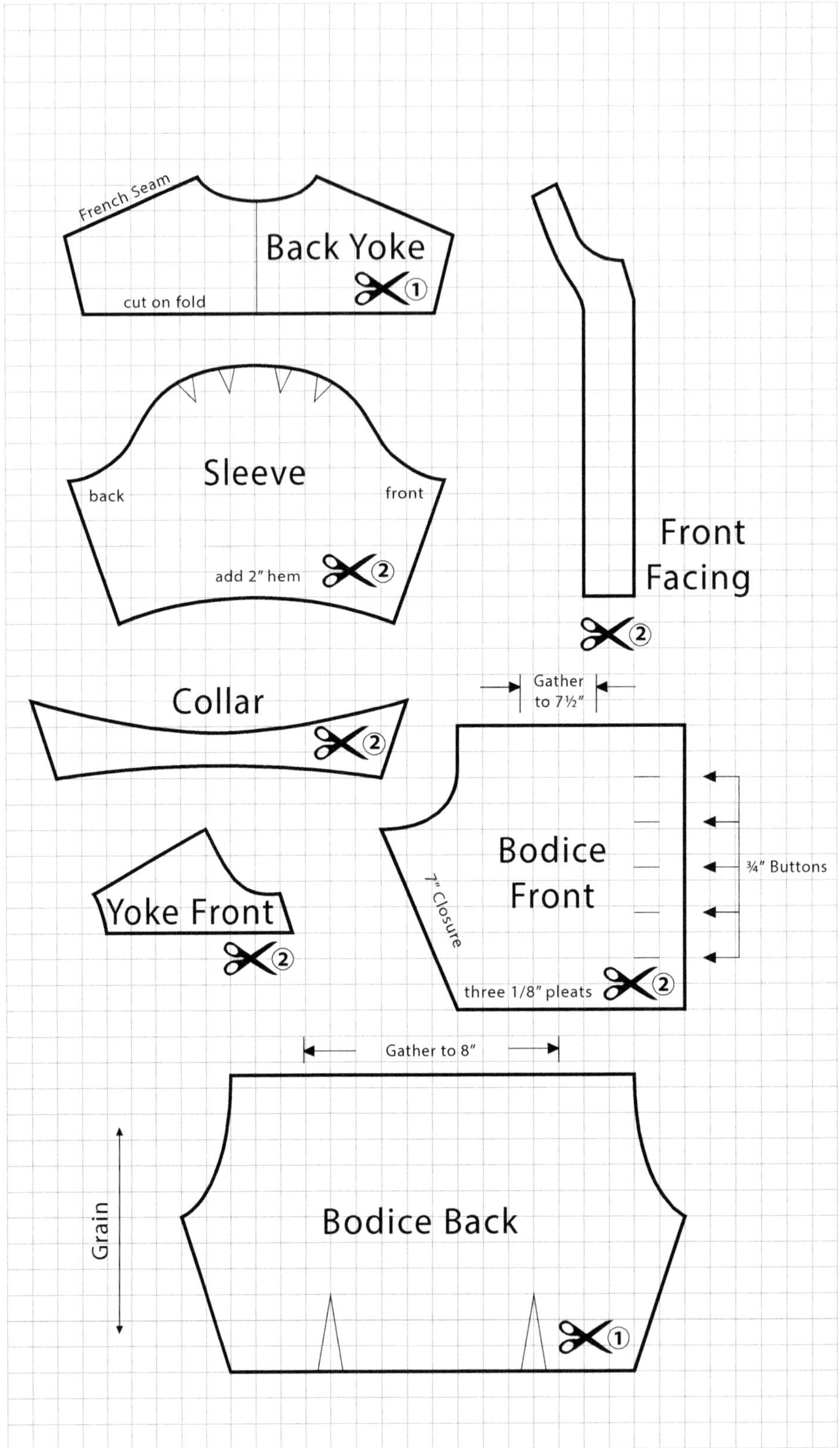
French Seam
Back Yoke
cut on fold
1
Sleeve
back
front
add 2″ hem
2
Front
Facing
2
Collar
2
Gather
to 7½″
Yoke Front
2
Bodice
Front
7″ Closure
¾″ Buttons
three 1/8″ pleats
2
Gather to 8″
Grain
Bodice Back
1

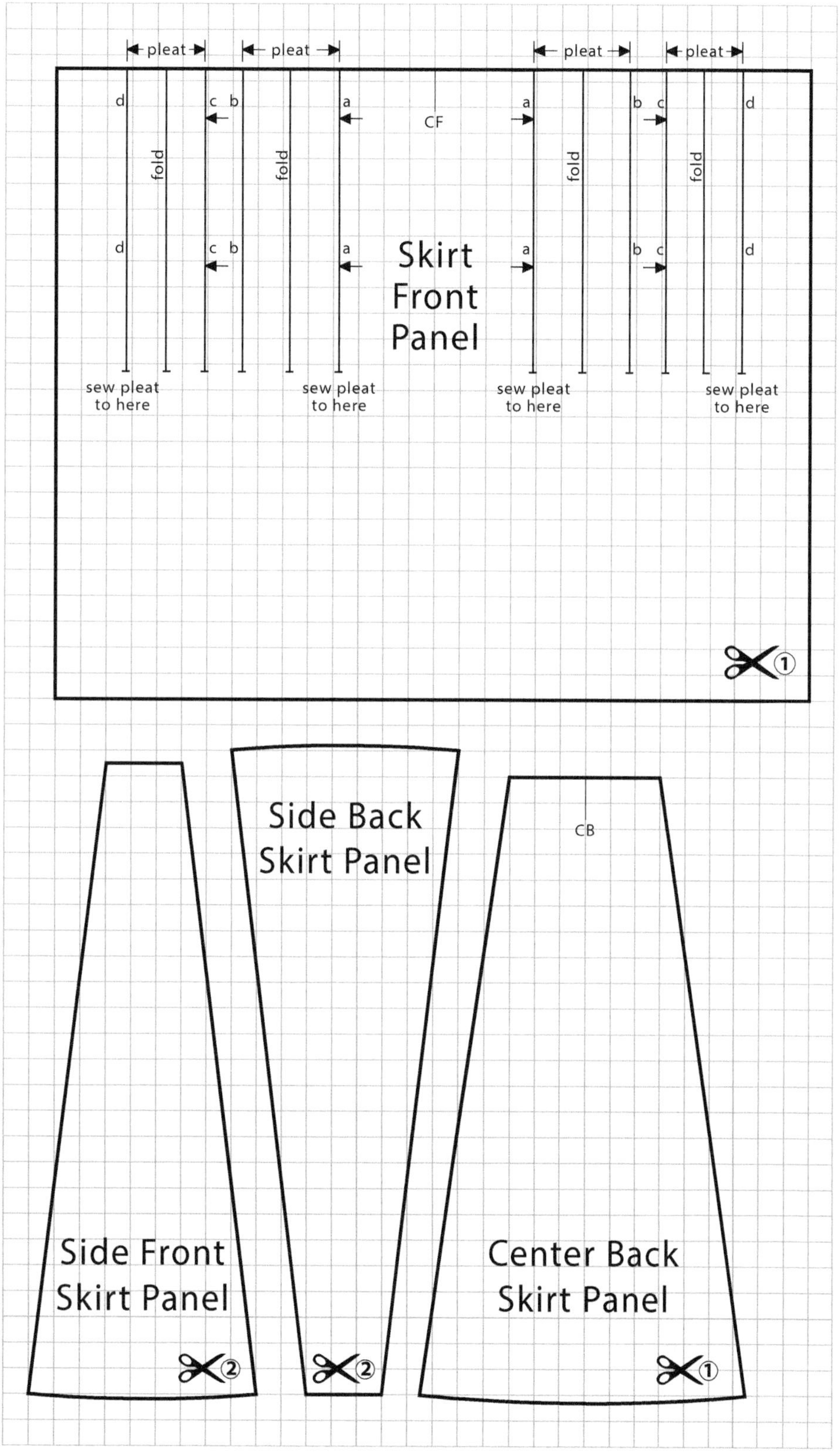
pleat
pleat
pleat
pleat
d
c b
a
CF
a
b c
d
fold
fold
fold
fold
Skirt Front Panel
sew pleat to here
sew pleat to here
sew pleat to here
sew pleat to here
①
Side Back Skirt Panel
CB
Side Front Skirt Panel
Center Back Skirt Panel
②
②
①

1954

Floral Brocade Evening Gown

The primary ambition of the post-WWII years was to get back to normal. Britain faced national shortages for years. Clothing austerity lasted until 1948 and food rationing continued until 1954.

The first post-war fashion delight was the reaction to the "New Look." In France, on February 12, 1947, the "season's sensation" was a new silhouette by Christian Dior. The war and its drab aftermath seemed to be over at last. The years of gloom, rationing, and uniforms were indeed overturned.

In Britain, during the autumn of 1947, several Royals were treated to a private showing of the Dior Collection at the French Embassy. By the end of the year the Dior silhouette appeared throughout England in ready-to-wear clothes. American women also eagerly adopted the new Dior style.

The "New Look" capitalized on the fashion nostalgia of a more traditionally feminine shape with sloping shoulders, prominent bust, narrow waist, full hips, and a mid-calf-length full skirt. This style dominated women's fashion until the late 1950s.

Blue brocade fabric

Dressmaker label

Skirt pleats

Bodice side

This evening gown is made of blue and white brocade with daisy-shaped flowers. It has a dressmaker's label from Ricci Michaels of Mayfair in London. As shown in the photograph, the dress was originally worn without straps. Sometime later someone added 1½-inch-wide shoulder straps.

The bodice has a square neckline that angles down at the back. The closure is a center back zipper that is finished at the top with a hook and

Bow

eye. The bodice is boned along the bust darts, along the side seams, and along the back darts.

The full floor length skirt has three pieces. The center front skirt is cut on the straight grain of the fabric and is gored and attached to the bodice without fullness. The wide back wedge pieces are cut along the length of the fabric and are knife-pleated all along the back of the bodice.

Bodice back

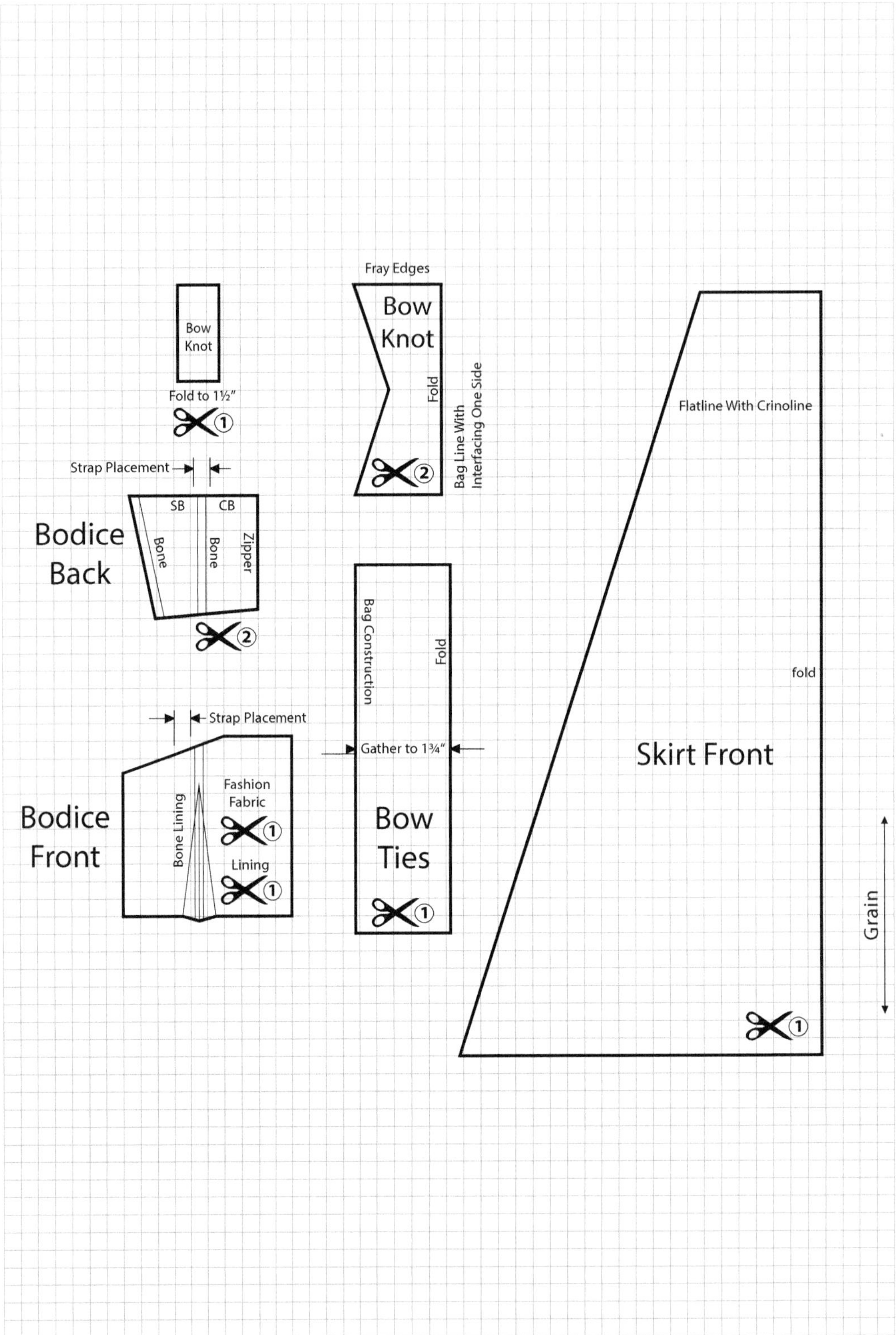
Bow
Knot
Fold to 1½″
1
Strap Placement
SB
CB
Bodice
Back
Bone
Bone
Zipper
2
Fray Edges
Bow
Knot
Fold
2
Bag Line With
Interfacing One Side
Bag Construction
Fold
Gather to 1¾″
Bow
Ties
1
Strap Placement
Bodice
Front
Bone Lining
Fashion
Fabric
1
Lining
1
Flatline With Crinoline
fold
Skirt Front
Grain
1

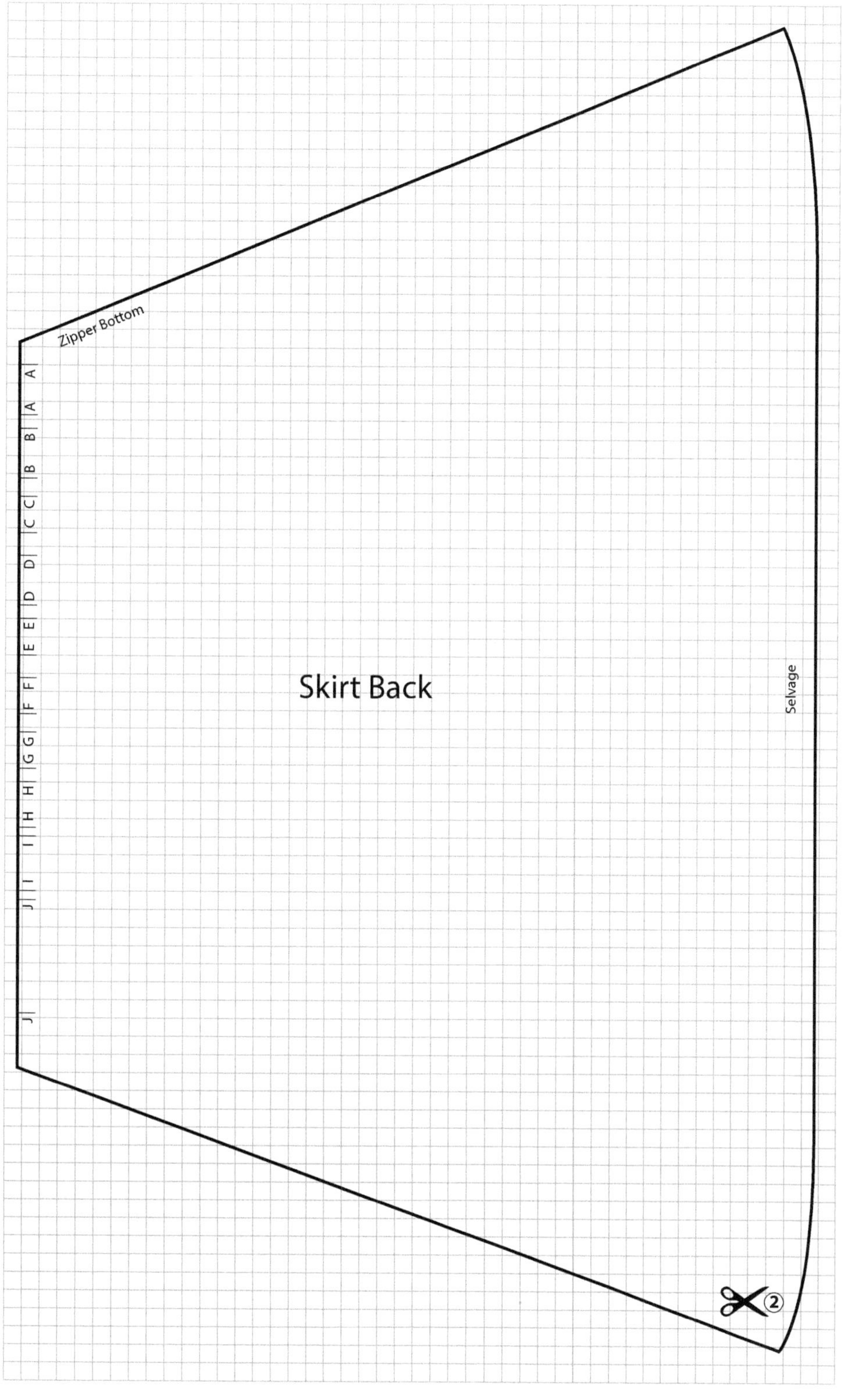
Zipper Bottom
A A
B B
C C
D D
E E
F F
G G
H H
I I
J J
Skirt Back
Selvage
2

I began to collect patterns from the Snowshill and Hereford historic clothing collections long before I knew what I was going to do with them. Althea Mackenzie suggested that I apply for the Society of Antiquaries *Janet Arnold Award*. Althea also suggested that I use the patterns to make full scale dresses. Theatre mockups, that are often made from plain muslin, came to mind. I was awarded the Janet Arnold grant in 2013. As a capstone the Society invited me to do a presentation of my work at a public lecture in London in May 2014. We decided at that lecture I would display the garments on live models.

Utah State University (USU), had an Interior Design Study Abroad program that would be in London during the time of my lecture. Darren Brooks of the USU Interior Design Faculty encouraged his students to participate in the project. I had 18 student volunteers. I limited the models to 11 and decided which dresses would be made and who would make them. I had three graduate students construct one each: Spencer Potter, Honji Zhu, and Mandolynn Browning. The remaining

Historical Dress: A Project Inspired by Janet Arnold – Society of Antiquaries, London, USU students and Nancy E. Hills , photo by Susie Tibbits

Tippetts Art Gallery, USU, Logan, UT

eight dresses were constructed by my longtime friend and colleague, Michelle Bradford. Whenever possible I had the garments made from white or cream fabrics as close to the original as I could. The 1945 utility dress was made from a rose-colored rayon crepe. I was able to find a white rayon crepe and make the new 1945 dress from that. Using similar fabrics allowed me to discover even more about the drape and texture of each garment. The monochromatic color scheme of this collection is deliberate. It allows the viewer to focus on the style lines of each garment. It also allows apparently unrelated garments to

Symphony in White,
Berrington Hall, Leominster, UK

Shades of White, Hereford Museum and Art Gallery

be seen as part of a whole.

We began in December of 2013 and had a trial run at USU during a Faculty Research presentation in April of 2014. The gowns dated from 1780 to 1945. I taught the models how to move in the dresses and gave them help with period hair styles. We all met one month later in London. I spent the day ironing the tightly packed gowns and had them ready for a performance of *Historical Dress: A Project Inspired by Janet Arnold* in May 2022. The small hall was filled. The 11 gowns were then packed up and taken to Berrington Hall, where they were on display for six months. That exhibit was named *Symphony in White*. I was invited to put the gowns on display in the Hereford Art Gallery in February of 2015. We added nine new gowns for a total of 20. The new gowns were dated from 1780–1954, and this exhibit was called *Shades of White*. Over the next four years I added 14 new gowns for a United States Institute of Theatre Technology presentation titled *Histories Mysteries*. During the

Tippetts Art Gallery, USU, Logan, UT,
photo by Doug Hills

summer of 2018, I was invited to display my research in London at the Society of Antiquaries *Unearthing the Past*, an interactive presentation of research with various Society of Antiquaries grant recipients. The most recent exhibit added another five new gowns, for a total of 39 on display at USU called *More Shades of White* spanning 1735 to 1954. I continue to gather patterns and I have another 20 patterns available that are yet to be constructed.

Tippetts Art Gallery, USU Students and
Nancy E. Hills, photo by Doug Hills

About the Author

Nancy E. Hills was born in a Studebaker in San Mateo, California. She is a Full Professor at Utah State University where she is head of the Theatre Costume Design program.

Photo by Dennis Hassan

Shows featuring her period piece designs include *Les Liaisons Dangereuses, Pride and Prejudice, To Kill a Mockingbird, The Miser, Enchanted April, Our Country's Good, Emma, Much Ado About Nothing, Anna Karenina, A Christmas Carol, The Moors, Pericles* and *Misalliance*. She has also designed at the Artist Repertory Theatre in Portland, Oregon including *Next to Normal, And So It Goes, The Playboy of the Western World* and *Blithe Spirit* and the Salt Lake Acting Company with productions of *Streetlight Woodpecker, Winter, Fun Home, Silent Dancer*, and *Hairy and Sherri.*

In 2013, Nancy gave a TEDxTalk, on the impact of WWII on clothing called *Make Do and Mend.* In March of 2023 Nancy gave a talk for the Spring Friends of the Merrill-Cazier Library Lecture Series based on the *Make Do and Mend* TEDxTalk. Also in 2013, Nancy was the recipient of the Janet Arnold Award from the Society of Antiquaries in London where she was funded to take patterns from two historic clothing collections in Herefordshire, UK. In July 2018, she was invited to present her historic pattern research at the Society of Antiquaries at *Unearthing the Past: Society of Antiquaries Research Showcase.* This project has grown into a collection of 50 white replicas of dresses taken from the patterns and shown in the United Kingdom and the United States in exhibits called *Symphony in White* and *Shades of White*. In 2018/2019 *More Shades of White* was on display in the USU Tippetts Gallery including 39 gowns from 1735–1954. Nancy returns to Herefordshire yearly to collect more information from historic garments. She has thus far accumulated 70+ patterns.

Website: www.nancyhillsdesign.com

About the Graphic Designer

Scott Nicklas is a graphic designer at Sports Training Systems in Portland, Oregon, where he specializes in developing educational materials for international gymnastics judges around the world. As a former gymnast and Oregon State University graduate with a BFA in Graphic Design, Scott has a unique blend of practical skills and knowledge in his field. His work is a primary source used to prepare judges for international events, including World Championships and the Olympic Games. His work has been published through both the International Gymnastics Federation's website and their magazine *We Are Gymnastics.*

Scott was introduced to Nancy E. Hills through her brother and Sports Training Systems' owner, Douglas Hills. In 2014, Scott designed graphic displays for Nancy's exhibits at the Society of Antiquaries, including *Symphony in White, Shades of White,* and *More Shades of White.*

Photo by Scott Nicklas

An aspiring author himself, Scott is in the process of writing his own novel, a fantasy novel set in a made-up world. Outside of work, Scott spends most of his free time discovering the world with his beautiful wife, Skye, and their two adorable children.

Website: scottnicklas.com

Glossary of Terms

applique	A sewing technique in which fabric pieces are layered on a foundation fabric, then stitched around the edges by hand or machine and covered with a decorative stitch. From the French "appliquer" (to put on).
armscye	Armhole opening in a garment.
Art Nouveau	An international style of the decorative arts, fine arts, and architecture that was popular between 1890 and 1910. Art Nouveau was inspired by natural forms, particularly the curved lines of vegetation and the movement of water.
artificial silk	When rayon (or viscose) was first introduced to clothing it was called artificial silk. Undoubtably to make it more sellable. Rayon is a synthetic fiber manufactured from the cellulose of wood pulp or cotton so it has the feel and look of natural fiber fabric.
Arts and Crafts	The Arts and Crafts movement began in the decorative and fine arts in 19th-century Britain and flourished internationally. The movement's figurehead, William Morris, had a notion that good design was linked to that of good society. This was a vision about the nature of work where the worker was not brutalized by harsh working conditions but could take pride in craftsmanship and skill. The Arts and Crafts movement encouraged traditional crafts skills, simple forms, and often used medieval, Romantic, or folk styles of decoration.
bag line	Sew around a hem (and possibly the sides), right sides together, one of the fashion fabric and one of the lining.
Bakst, Léon	(1866–1924) A Russian painter, scenic and costume designer for Diaghilev and the Russian Ballet. He was known for exotic, richly colored sets and costumes reminiscent of *The Arabian Nights*.
bateau (neckline)	A bateau neck or boat neck, a wide neckline that runs across collarbone from shoulder point to shoulder point.
bias	The bias grain of woven fabric 45 degrees to its warp and weft threads.
bias band	Bias tape or bias binding is a narrow strip of fabric, cut on the bias.

block print	To print from hand-cut wooden blocks.
bodice	The part of a woman's garment (excluding sleeves) that is above the waist.
bottine	A dress boot.
box pleat	Two knife pleats facing each other.
brocade	A woven, patterned fabric using multi-colored threads. A raised pattern in relief against the background.
burnished	A shiny, metallic quality.
calamanco	Plain or patterned wool of Flemish or English manufacture, sometimes part silk or goat hair.
calico fabric	a. Cotton cloth originally imported from Calicut in Southern India. b. British: a plain white cotton fabric that is heavier than muslin. c. US: various inexpensive cotton fabrics with figured patterns.
cap (sleeve)	A sleeve extending only a short distance from the shoulder and tapering to nothing under the arm.
caraco	A style of informal woman's jacket that was worn from the mid-18th century and often made of printed linen or cotton. Caracos were usually thigh-length and opened in front, with three-quarter or long sleeves and the back could be fitted to the waist or hang in a "sack-back."
cartridge pleat	Used to gather a large amount of fabric into a small waistband, yoke or armscye. This type of pleating also allows the fabric to spring out from the seam. Each pleat is tightly whipstitched onto a waistband or into an armscye.
CC41	The British austerity scheme for conserving and providing clothing and house hold goods during WWII, "Civilian Clothing 1941."
chemisette	An article of women's clothing worn to fill in the front and neckline of any garment. Chemisettes give the appearance of a blouse or shirt worn under the outer garment without adding bulk at the waist or upper arm.

couching	Embroidering a heavy thread laid on the surface of fabric and sewed down with stitches of another thread.
crepe, finish fabric	A weave property or fabric treatment method that results in a rippling, three-dimensional texture. The rose-colored 1945 dress was made from a rayon crepe. Rayon was also used to fill the needs of cotton, wool, and silk during the WWII fabric shortages.
crinoline	A stiff fabric made of horsehair and cotton or linen and used for underskirts. By the early 1850s it was the name of the silhouette from horsehair petticoats, and later of the hoop skirts that replaced them in the mid-1850s.
dart	Folds sewn into fabric to tuck in and shape a garment.
Dior, Christian	(1905–1957) Head of a French fashion house that brought recognition to a more traditional feminine silhouette of the post-World War II era with his "New Look," revitalizing *haute couture* in Paris.
Dorset button	Originally made from a disc cut from the horn of a Dorset sheep and wrapped with thread.
drawstrings	A string, cord, lace, or rope used to "draw" (gather, or shorten) fabric or other material usually through a hem or casing.
fashion fabric	The nicer fabric used for the outside of a garment.
flatline	Cut pattern piece from a support fabric and attach it to fashion fabric. The double layer is then treated as one piece in the garment construction.
flounces (lace)	Ruffles of linen, cotton or lace, often attached inside of elbow length sleeves. Could be removed for cleaning. Flounces are also called *engageantes*.
gauze	Thin fabrics of silk, linen or cotton.
Gibson, Charles Dana	An American graphic artist, best known for his creation of the Gibson Girl, an iconic representation of the beautiful and independent American woman at the turn of the 20th century.
gimp	A narrow braided or twisted ornamental trim.

gored panel	A triangular panel of fabric with the top of the triangle cut off resulting in a long trapezoid often used for a skirt. This shape eliminates the excess fabric at the waist while providing fullness at the hem.
grain	The lengthwise and crosswise threads of woven fabrics. When there is a grain direction on a pattern the arrow follows the lengthwise threads.
grosgrain	Fabric or ribbon characterized by its weft (lengthwise) is heavier than its warp (cross-grain), creating prominent lengthwise ribs much like cording.
habit (riding)	An outfit for horseback riding.
hooped petticoat	A women's undergarment worn in various periods to hold the skirt into a fashionable shape. Hoopskirt petticoats consisted of a fabric petticoat sewn with channels to serve as casings for stiffening like whalebone, steel, or rope.
horsehair	Fabric or braid woven with wefts of tail hair from horses and cotton or silk warps. Horsehair fabrics are sought for durability. This stiffener was used to give body to hemlines and puff sleeves.
knife pleat	A sharp pleat on a garment made in one direction and typically overlapping another. Knife pleats that face each other form one box pleat.
madder	A red dye or pigment obtained from the root of the madder plant, or a synthetic dye resembling it. Madder dyes typically included red-black, red, pink, and purple.
mantua	Originally a loose late 17th-century gown where the bodice and skirt were joined and opened up the front. Often closed over a stomacher. A woman's dressmaker came to be known as a mantua maker. It was worn through most of the 18th century.
Morris, William	(1834–1896) A British 19th-century artist, craftsman, designer, poet, and visionary thinker: "Have nothing in your houses that you do not know to be useful or believe to be beautiful." Morris had a huge impact on the British Socialist and Arts and Crafts movements.
mother of pearl	The hard, pearly, iridescent substance that forms the inner layer of a mollusk shell. Often used for jewelry, buttons, etc.

Mucha, Alphonse	(1860–1939) A Czech Art Nouveau painter. He was an artist known for his illustrations of women used in advertisements, decorative panels, designs, and theatrical posters, which became among the most iconic images of the period.
muslin	A cotton fabric of plain weave and various weights. It gets its name from the city of Mosul, Iraq where it may have been originally manufactured. It was imported into Europe for much of the 17th and early 18th centuries.
pelerines	A woman's cape of lace or silk with pointed ends at the center front, popular in the mid-19th century.
pelisse	A fashionable style of women's coat worn in the early 19th century.
pencilled	Early 19th-century laying on of colors by hand on printed fabrics. By 1830, the use of pencilling had died out, as more economical means of applying color were available.
peplum	A short flounce or extension of a garment below the waist, covering the hips.
petersham	A heavy interfacing band to give body to a waistband or belt.
petticoat	An underskirt often seen at the front opening of a skirt and later an underskirt to give body to the shape of a skirt.
pin ground	Finely outlined patterns achieved by means of metal strips and pins inserted into wood blocks used for printing.
pin tucks	Small tucks or pleats, especially multiple parallel tucks, used to shape or decorate clothing. When tucks are very narrow, they are called pin tucks or pin-tucking.
piping	Embellishment consisting of a strip of folded fabric inserted into seam to define the edges or style lines of a garment. Usually the fabric strip is cut on the bias.
Poiret, Paul	(1879–1944) A leading French fashion designer and master couturier during the early 20th century. He claimed responsibility for ridding women of the corset, as well as introducing the hobble skirt, harem pants and the lampshade skirt.
polonaise	An overskirt (late 18th century) draped up at the sides to prevent from trailing on the ground.

pre-Raphaelite	A group of British 19th-century artists (the Pre-Raphaelite Brotherhood) including Hunt, Millais, and Rossetti, were inspired by Italian art of the 14th and 15th century. They appreciated the uncomplicated depiction of nature in Italian painting before Raphael. The Brotherhood's active life lasted five years but its influence on painting, decorative arts, and interior design was extensive.
princess line	A fitted garment cut in long panels without a horizontal seam at the waist. The fit is achieved with long seams and shaped pattern pieces. The princess line was introduced by Charles Frederick Worth in the early 1870s and named in honor of the tall, lean, and elegant Princess Alexandra.
raglan (sleeves)	A type of sleeve where the top is part of the neck opening. The top side of the sleeve has a diagonal seam from underarm to collarbone and the underarm seam goes from armpit to edge finish.
rayon	A cellulous fiber usually made from wood pulp. It is a versatile fabric with the capability to imitate other fabrics. Rayon has taken on properties similar to silk, cotton, or wool. Modal, cupro, and lyocell are some of the names for rayon. In the 1920s, rayon was known as artificial silk.
revers	An early version of lapels.
riding habit	Clothing for horseback riding.
roller print	A mechanical development where a pattern was etched into copper rollers and gave manufacturers the ability to print larger quantities fabric at greater speed, at lower prices, making the production of cotton prints increase in the late 18th and early 19th century.
ruching	Fabric or trim gathered either down the center or along the two outside edges.
sack-back gown	The sack-back gown or robe à la française was an 18th-century women's fashion. In the early 18th century, the sack-back gown was a very informal style. The gown had large back box pleats which fell loose from the shoulder to the floor, sometimes with a small train. It was usually closed in the front over a stomacher and showing a petticoat.

sartorial	Used to refer to any matter pertaining to the consideration of clothing or fashion.
selvage	The tightly woven finished side edges of fabric as it comes off of the loom. The selvage edges prevent the fabric from unraveling.
shawl collar	A rounded turned-down collar, without lapel notches, that extends down the front of a garment.
Singer, Isaac	(1811–1875) An American inventor, actor, and entrepreneur. Singer invented the first practical, commercially-successful sewing machine and was the founder of the Singer Sewing Machine Company, one of the first multi-national American businesses.
stays	An 18th-century boned undergarment. Stays formed the torso into a stiff, inverted cone, raising and supporting the bust, and providing a solid foundation on which garments fit.
surplice front	A front bodice closure that crosses over the front and is attached at the side.
sutache	A narrow, flat, ornamental braid used to trim garments.
tricorn	A hat whose brim is turned up on three sides, usually made of felt, straw, or buckram.
twill tape	A flat twill-woven ribbon of cotton. It may be used to reinforce seams, make casings, bind edges, and make sturdy ties for garment closures.
utility	Due to the shortage of clothing materials and labor during WWII, the British Board of Trade created a range of "utility clothing" meeting specific regulations used in construction. Utility clothing was marked with a CC41 label.
velvet	A fabric with a thick soft pile of short erect threads; sometimes a similar woolen cloth, later silk and rayon.
waistband	A separate band of fabric that encircles the waist of a skirt, trousers, or bottom of a bodice.
yoke	A separate piece of the shoulder and neck of a shirt or bodice.

Bibliography

Arnold, Janet. *Patterns of Fashion I: Englishwomen's Dresses and Their Construction c. 1660–1860*. New York: Drama Book Publishers, 1977.

Arnold, Janet. *Patterns of Fashion I: Englishwomen's Dresses and Their Construction c. 1860–1940*. New York: Drama Book Publishers, 1991.

Ashelford, Jane. *The Art of Dress: Clothes and Society 1500–1914*. New York: Harry N. Abrams, 1996.

Batterberry, Michael. *Mirror, Mirror: A Social History of Fashion*. New York: Holt, Rinehart and Winston, 1977.

Baumgarten, Linda. *Eighteenth-Century Clothing at Williamsburg*. Williamsburg, VA: The Colonial Williamsburg Foundation, 1986.

Baumgarten, Linda and Watson, John and Carr, Florine. *Costume Close-up*, Clothing Construction and Pattern, 1750–1790. Williamsburg, VA: The Colonial Williamsburg Foundation, 1999.

Boucher, François. *20,000 Years of Fashion: The History of Costume and Personal Adornment*. New York: Harry N. Abrams, 1967.

Bradfield, Nancy. *Costume in Detail: Women's Dress 1730–1930*. Boston: Plays, Inc., 1968.

Cunnington, C. Willett, *English Women's Clothing in the Present Century*. London: Faber & Faber, 1952.

Cunnington, C. Willett and Cunnington, Phillis. *Handbook of English Costume in the 18th Century*. London: Faber & Faber, 1957.

Cunnington, C. Willett and Cunnington, Phillis. *Handbook of English Costume in the 18th Century*. Boston: Plays, Inc., 1972.

Green, Susan W., *Wearable Prints, 1760–1860, History, Materials, and Mechanics*. Kent, OH: Kent University Press, 2014.

Hamlyn, Paul, *The Pictorial Encyclopedia of Fashion*, New York: Crown Publishers, 1968.

Kyoto Costume Institute. *Revolution in Fashion 1715–1815*. New York: Abbeville Press, 1989.

MacKenzie, Althea. *Buttons and Trimmings*. London: National Trust, 2005a.

MacKenzie, Althea. *Embroideries*. London: National Trust, 2005b.

Ribeiro, Aileen. *The Art of Dress: Fashion in England and France 1750–1820.* New Haven, CT and London: Yale University Press, 1997.

Rothstein, Natalie (Ed.). *A Lady of Fashion: Barbara Johnson's Album of Styles and Fabrics.* Lond: Thames and Hudson, 1987.

Rothstein, Natalie (Ed.). *Four Hundred Years of Fashion.* London: Victoria and Albert Museum, in association with William Collins, 1984.

Tozer, Jane and Levitt, Sarah. *Fabric of Society: A Century of People and Their Clothes 1770-1870.* Powys, Wales: Laura Ashley Limited, 1983.

Walford, Jonathan. *Forties Fashion: From Siren Suits to the New Look.* London: Thames & Hudson, 2008.

Waugh, Nora. *Corsets and Crinolines.* London: Batsford, 1954.

Waugh, Norah, *The Cut of Women's Clothes, 1600–1930.* London: Faber & Faber, 1968.

Index

Locators in *italic* indicate figures.